# For the Adult Daughters of Evil
Fake, Disre
Wishy-Was|                                            |,
Self-Righte
Toxic, Never Satisfied, Manipulative,
and Unsupportive Faux-Mothers!

# BLACK CAT

## <u>1</u>

A mother who is both and enemy and rival
Can make a sane daughter suicidal
Shared DNA makes our mothers feel entitled
They say that our disease lives in us because we don't pray
enough and don't follow *her* twisted gospel
And just the stench from her critiques burn my nostrils
Your mother acts like she's the 13th disciple
And no matter how much she and her Terracotta Warriors
quote the Bible
She and her minions sound more and more illogical
And she'll betray you like Pontius Pilate and Judas in the
Bible.

I call them Terracotta Warriors
Terracotta Warriors are the individuals who pretend to care
about you
But are underhandedly positioned to always defend the cruelty
and deceptions of your evil mother.

Her misguided Terracotta Warriors are merely funerary art

Designed and specifically erected by her to rip your quest for
freedom, truthfulness and happiness apart
And the role of the spineless mouthpiece is their favorite part
And any battle for your "mother" they always start
And the unfair lies they tell about you and I are off the charts
She never takes responsibility for her actions and the mean
things she barks
Yet, we get unfairly blamed for upsetting the apple cart.


Like the thousands and thousands of Terracotta Warriors
guarding Emperor Qin's tomb
She erects her brainwashed and weak-minded accomplices to
protect her from any impending doom.

Today's Terracotta Warriors exist in places other than China
You tend to see them whenever you exercise your right to
honesty and happiness as a daughter
She'll deploy her brainless Terracotta Warriors to intimidate
you in hope of evoking shudder.

Her Terracotta Warriors work hypnotically and mistakenly for
her
So whatever your opinion or stance is
Never expect them to sympathize, empathize or concur.

The actual Terracotta Warriors in China are powerless edicts
of clay and stone
Daughter, stand up against her ridiculousness and tyranny
Even if you must confront her lying and meanness all alone
Speak the pain you know.

Emperor Qin constructed the Terracotta Warriors for his
afterlife
Today, you've been given the opportunity to unapologetically
live your own life
You've been given another precious opportunity to purposely
get it right
So don't allow her to systematically ruin your tremendous
opportunity twice.

And just because her Terracotta Warriors may be blood they
ain't nothing nice
They'll come for you no matter the price
Their defense of her cruelty and meanness isn't right
Recognize that she's your spiritual and emotional kryptonite
She'll intentionally try to sabotage any goal or aspiration you
have within your sight
You and I
We know what evil-ass mothers are really like
Their lips are made of toxic waste so they can't kiss you
goodnight
To be happy, dear daughter
You have the right
You know what her Terracotta Warriors and minions are like
Stop being scared and stop being polite
Her energy-sucking vampires don't have to wait until midnight
Those positivity-draining vampires have even found a way to
move in sunlight
Their conscious should be heavy
But yours shall remain light.


## 2

I sit on my throne
I survive it even with Multiple Sclerosis, as you know
I stay focused and I stay quietly in my zone
Yet, she won't leave me alone
We rise time and time again while listening to Sting's *Fields of
Gold*
Yet, jealousy is all she can show
The adult daughters out there know
That no matter how successful we are
Resentment she will only show
And every plan we share with her
She proceeds to tell us that it's a no-go
And when we do what is best for ourselves
We never get her vote
Because God told her so
I know I'm not alone

The men feel it when their wives come home
Or maybe that partner or girlfriend detects that something is
wrong
Your girl is upset and you can figure out what's going on
Only to learn that she is once again pissed by what has been
boiling under the surface all along
With her mother she just got off the phone
And to that evil woman
She'll be forever a child and never grown
She's an adult that her mother likes to scold
And her mother takes, takes, takes, because she feels she is
owed
So the upset outbursts and tears
We adult daughters are always prone
And the people we love the most are predisposed
To the madness we feel what our mothers won't leave us
alone
And you wonder why I'm gone.

3

The camera often never reflects the best in daughters...often
me
Especially
My life with her has always been like a perpetual selfie
Every day the *Truman Show* we were making
Mentally taping and verbally recording so it could be used
against me
My own mother
Oh, what cruelty!
The affirmation and encouragement I was always seeking
From a person that was never going to be giving
Life with her has always been phony
Staged like a selfie because she found sincerity annoying
Everything the world saw was misleading
You never really saw me
Just what my parents wanted you to believe
And what they coordinated for you to see
And just because one sees me
Doesn't mean that one knows me

She was the original paparazzi
Always watching and stalking and trying to trap me
Young daughters, be careful of what you are showing
The repercussions can be ongoing
Talk to an adult daughter who is knowing
Too far you could already be going
In a selfie what do you see?
I never really see you
And you may never really see me
Especially when we are both pretending and adjusting the lighting
And before you know it,
You are like my mother and you are lying
Covering
If it was reflected back to you in a frame or on a screen I was likely faking
How could it be called a selfie?
When I never see myself in me.


## 4

*Unbought and Unbossed* like Shirley Chisolm
I'm fully aware of my family's dogmatic sexism and schism
Which flows through "sanctified" mothers who oppress other women
My mother views women and daughters through a really weird prism
Being her daughter means you live in a psychological prison
Never authorized or equipped to make a real decision
And when you start to escape her delusion
She calls on her Terracotta Warriors to bring you back into submission
Freedom? Own choices? Don't you dare reference the situation!
So my true plans I NEVER mention
Like this book,
No one saw it commin'
Evil mothers,

It's time to start runnin'!

## 5

According to Greek mythology
I'm ruled by Mercury
The only zodiac sign representing femininity
My sapphire can be clearly seen
I epitomize helpfulness and reliability
And she must not realize that Virgos have spectacular
memories
So, I'll never forget the evil perpetrated against me
And her devious intentions I view critically
And her dogma and twisted mentality
Removes her from reality
And I'm much too sane to allow her phoniness and craziness
to exist around me
Nothing she is, is who I want to be
She calls herself family
But I call my mother the enemy.

## 6

I never wanted to say it
But she poked and instigated
She does it time and time again because it's tolerated
They always allow her to get away with it
She's the reason the daughters are medicated
I know what she's insinuated
She never takes responsibility for her actions
And falsely declares that the truth is all hallucinated
She never recalls it
She is a religious sorcerer who destroys truths like magic
No longer will I allow my life be delegated
She is no longer allowed to dictate it
I've done nothing wrong yet she criticizes it
I always try to do the right thing and she unfairly judges it
Even when it is for my betterment
My happiness and advancement
She's tragic

Her camouflaged jealousy is toxic
My life's course I now direct it
Her same ole' judgments and biblical psychobabble is
syndicated
The constant replays and relentless reruns leave me
nauseated
I'm tired of hearing it
I won't permit it
I will no longer suffer through it
My emotions are complicated
But it's MY life
And I'ma live it!

7

To accept that your mother is a cold-hearted witch
But you have the right to truthfully say it
So what if her minions can't handle it
Who gives a shit?
Don't be ashamed to declare it
And let the world know it
Her niceties they believe it
Because she's great at being as phony as they get.

8

She's leaving her writing class
In the car she's listening to **Waves** by Joey Bada$$
And until she arrives she knows the peacefulness will last
But once her mother's flight arrives all happiness will soon
pass.

In her guest room she dreads just allowing her to lay
She wishes it didn't have to be this way
But that has never been the case
In the daughter's spirit the anxiety and discomfort stays
The daughter can only deal with her mother for no more than
an hour or so these days
Despite what the forced smile on her face may say
The daughter doesn't really feel that way.

They're talking about him and the many, many accusations
against him on TV today
And as the daughter looks away
She wishes she could say
That she too knows how someone's daughter becomes prey
Confessions often happen over long periods of time and
many, many days
They'll believe the altar boys but never what we say
And she understands why they couldn't speak it out loud until
today
She knows what it is like when it is too late to pray
And the visions remind you every day
And as the daughter hears some bullshit about some
"tarnished legacy" she heard someone in denial say
She gets pissed watching other women excuse the evidence
away.

Because that's what some talking heads had the audacity to
say
Failing to recognizing that sometimes wisdom and courageous
doesn't manifest itself for decades
Why should any victimized women feel ashamed?
Back in 2007, Nikki Giovanni tried to tell us back then that he
was crazy and a damn shame
Guess he didn't know that those kinds of repeated evil acts
eventually become balls and chains
He had to know that it coming one day
He had to know that karma was headed his way
I believe that he drugged and sexually assaulted and raped
them matter what the deniers say
There ain't no way that everybody is lying
His excuses don't hold water like a cracked ice tray
When I see him I see a serial rapists like my daddy
And I see my mother standing by like nothing is happening.

Many years ago Nikki Giovanni called him out and his
troubling behaviors out by name
We see the umbrellas and then we are shocked when it
actually rains

Nikki Giovanni, I am a motherless and fatherless daughter,
and I can surely say
Thank you for speaking out that day
For having the courage to say what others refuse to say
Doubters should listen to his pound cake speech claims
After that decide if you still feel the same way?
He got a lot of nerve, I say!
And listen to his spanish fly standup routine where he
discusses drugging women, okay
With amnesia and denial so many are plagued
*What's Happening* has always been my favorite anyway
Shout out to Dr. Danielle Spencer, my favorite veterinarian I
must say
And just listening to folks defend him only affirms why I love
animals more than humans anyway.

<u>9</u>

Often we need our distance to be far enough away
And even if she is close in proximity
"Mother" isn't a word we feel comfortable ever saying
And for us sometimes no contact is necessary to get us
through each day
And begging God to change her we can no longer pray
It hasn't worked anyway
The evil hasn't changed forms and it's still the same
If safety is truly first as they say
Keep her far, far away.

<u>10</u>

She's a walking minstrel show
Who in the hell told her that was okay?
Hell, we don't know
Authenticity isn't a put-on and take-off role
Realness doesn't come and go
How's that something that you don't know?
You're a fraud you know?

Sometimes the only thing left to do is to go!
Those thievery and deceptive tactics and too much she has gleefully stole!
It is annoying when the deceiver tries to lecture the duped on what they *think* they know
Even with your fabricated map you can't properly navigate this here road
I don't know what you've been told
But you have long overstayed your welcome and it's time for you to go!
You are in our home and we say so
That disrespectful behavior is a no-go!
If my mother was a man, they'd tell that a should have dumped his emotionally abusive ass long, long ago
And to her costume and masquerade party we will be no-shows
If anyone asks you for a statement like you're some sort of pro
Please be like DARE and "just say no"
And refer any inquiry you may receive to the experienced experts who really know
Because you DON'T know
Our birthright for you is just some silly blackface show
The reality and density of melanin and gender can't be made up as you go
You clearly don't care to know!

11

Think of all the things that she tried to stop you from doing
Remember all of the happiness that she tried to stop you from pursuing?
Do you recall all of the wonderful things she said you shouldn't be having?
Your independence and gaiety she was dedicated to ruining
All along knowing exactly what she was intentionally doing
But you kept your goals in mind and kept it moving
You got what you wanted and you kept on improving
You were better than good, but for her there was never enough proving

She enters a room and immediately your stomach starts
moving
The contents in your gut start churning
Whatever she cannot take credit for she is quickly undoing
When your mother doubles as your hater and her jealousy and
envy is brewing
She will never be loving and any temporary calm is never
enduring
She will never-ever be approving
The chaos is always of her doing.

## 12

You don't lie or cheat or steal
Yet, she always has a problem with you
And never with them.

With absolute toxic masculinity and sexist power
The men in the family can do what they want
The get DUI's, use disrespectful vulgarities to describe
woman, stay drunk, constantly cheat on their girlfriends, and
all-day smoke blunts
But we haven't done anything wrong and she attacks us.

Narcissistic mothers hate daughters who are better than them
Our positive outlook they view as a sin
Because what they didn't have the courage to do we did
And mothers like ours hate it
Because everything we said we'd do we followed through with
it
So now they're jealous.

She never complains about the womanizing and mistreatment
of women by her sons
She'll hug the mistress and smile at the long-term-girlfriend
one
You know the kind of mother who never checks immorality in
her sons
Because she only pretends to have some
Fronting like she never went down that road

Intimidating and bullying us because we don't care who is told
But when it comes to her daughter
Ya'll already know
She rules through frightening dogma and "because I say so"
Even when her daughter is grown.

As long as you are a man
No matter how mean and deceptive and untrustworthy you are
She becomes an unwavering supporter and ardent fan
Of almost any integrity deprived and controlling man
Balls are far more important than ovaries in her eyes
She is a sexist and an oppressive woman who will lie
She's worse than a chauvinistic man any time
Sometimes mothers are far worse than a disrespectful and
misogynistic man anytime
Because they do way more damage and cross way more
lines.

13

Be bold.
Do not buy into what you've been told.
In creativity, intelligence and inner beauty you shall be
clothed
You mother doesn't believe in you but remember you've been
told
Do not allow her to reconstruct your mold
And never drive on her unpaved road
Whatever it is that you want to accomplish please, please grab
hold
Don't let it go
The daughters are with you
You are not in this alone
If she can't respect you,
Don't allow that disrespectful woman back into your home.

14

Once I stopped condoning the generational lie I was required
to mimic

I was able to walk away from my biggest cynic
I was able to detach from the maternal drama and madness
that is always in orbit
Every fault and personal obstacle, I could freely admit
I learned to distance myself from her judgment
And I stopped adjusting my stance and behavior just to
appease my family critics
And if she said it, I learned to bravely reject it.

### 15

Why are we always surprised?
A lying mother will always lie
Save your tears because she won't care if you cry
She will definitely come up with some far-fetched excuse or
impossible alibi
We may never understand the reason why
But stop being surprised when she uses her fangs to actually
bite.

### 16

You will never be whole
Until you acknowledge that inner hole
You didn't allow her to subdue your soul
With every gut punch and criticism you learned to roll
You discovered maternal love elsewhere when she refused
the critical role
You became a heroic giant when she tried to make you a puny
gnome.

### 17

I'm proud of myself
And anyone who isn't

Go eff' yourself!
Yeah, I said it!
And I meant it!
I told the truth
I put up with the emotional abuse
She used her dogma and pious attitude as a noose
My wisdom and success were never enough proof
That's why there will never be a truce
There is now too much for me to lose
And my peace would be disturbed if I let her once more
misuse
For her two cents, I have absolutely no use
She can't be fixed and I've retraced the clues
She's too corrupt and mean to be around me or you
Her opinion is irrelevant now
As long as I approve.


## 18

If I could count every tear
Every snide remark and every sneer
Acceptance so far away, but ridicule always so near
She's always claiming that the best mother is here
Learning to oblige only out of desperation and utter fear
You can still see her fading image in the rear
Your condemnation is always closer than it appears
After finally absolving yourself from her, you had to cheer
But the suffering of a daughter at the hands of the faux-
maternal can only be calculated in dog years
I understand that, My Dear.

## 19

She's so emotionally and financially abusive and draining
For honesty and love we are always waiting
We do all the giving and she does all the taking

The emotionally and physically abused daughters everywhere
know what I'm saying
She's the faux-Christian that is always complaining
And somehow convinced you that happiness and peace is
worth delaying
Her oppressive and sexist rules we are forced into obeying
And we endure unjustifiable shaming
Be kind to yourself
She's the one you should be blaming.

## 20

I know what your family is like.
A sincere apology is never your right.
Everyone is acting phony just to be polite.
Getting to the truth is like untangling damn Christmas lights.
Everyone pointing fingers and claiming that the other isn't
right.
Despite your disguised anger you pretend like everything is
alright
But everyone is a liar and can't be trusted in your line of sight.
When surrounded by that many shady people going no
contact is your right.
All of the underhandedness done out of pure spite.
But one more insult from your mother and you will surely
ignite!
She'll antagonize you until you divulge your gripes.
She will never sympathize with you are respect your plight.
But she plays the well-rehearsed roll of the victim after every
instigated fight.
You've held your tongue with all your might
But you will finally let that evil witch know how you felt tonight
I know what your family is like

You are always wrong
And she is always, always right.

21

I get it
She isn't some prized motherly relic
You have learned to be the skeptic
Sometimes you wonder if you will ever get over it
So I have converted our pain into the poetic
Do not believe that her curses are prophetic
Realize that her negative energy is frenetic
You are strong and you are undefined by the pathetic
She has proven to be negligent
I understand that leaving was for your own betterment
She is not prolific
You asked her for the emotional specific and she ignored it
You will never be able to make her different
It isn't possible to authenticate the counterfeit.

22

Sometimes a daughter has to finally walk away
When she can't respect your man or your partner I say
You best get away!
And when we tell the truth on any given day
We have to endure and listen to someone else's dismay
We have to listen to the ridiculous advice of someone who
isn't tied to the pain
We always gotta listen to every what's his name and the
bullshit they claim
Dummies acting like experts anyway
Terracotta Warriors are always generationally in training
They know the many stories surrounding what you've been
saying
But they never want the daughter to begin naming
Because it is the mother her minions are protecting
And all ignore the terror the daughter has been exclaiming
But thus comes the day of reckoning!

You can't stop me from writing
And even though daughters are forgiving
In our lives our mothers can't be participating
Because allowing her in permits only more anxiety
And her insults she will continue supplying
Cruel words will begin flying
And on your pain she will begin capitalizing
Even sadistically applauding
And the misery we will keep internalizing
We've tried countless times but her presence is terrorizing
Daughter, the truth is visible so stop denying.

### 23

When something is suffering truly
We say, "Put it out of its misery"
Well, we did just that to end our own torturing you see
We put to rest a relationship that she was dedicated to
destroying
Why is our torment acceptable and not believed?
Why is our distress and pain not considered abnormal cruelty?
Why is it okay that we are suffering?
Just because it is at the hands of our mothers doesn't mean
that her behavior society is worth condoning
Or excusing.

### 24

My mother loves picking it up
Analyzing it
And declaring that from her I stole it!
Because if it's nice she says that *from her* I took and stole it
Because even when it is mine
She doesn't believe that I deserve it
A picture in MY fame in MY house, that I took
And she'll claim that from *her* I secretly snatched it!
And without her permission I stole it!

So before she arrives bringing her false accusations and havoc
I go through my house taking down things because of her ridiculousness accusations and childish antics
"Oh, you know how she is" they say always dismissing it
And her evil-ass once again gets acquitted
I just don't get it
Daughters raise your hand if your mother also does it.


We make it
They steal it
Then charge us quadruple to reclaim it
Now they've acquired it
Now they get to rebrand it
Repackage it
So that they own it now and the originator isn't credited
As long as it translates into a paycheck
And shady family members are cool with it
They'll rob you of it
And then call their stolen acquisitions "blessings" like it just appeared like magic
And sometimes mothers are the masterminds behind it
Tragic.


<u>25</u>


Once I kill a person off in my mind
They are no longer alive
And they don't reemerge at a later time
The women I admire the most are those who know themselves inside
Shout out to the women who refuse to suffer just because they became his bride
Shout out to the mothers who support their daughters through divorce or separation and for them those mothers ride
Shout out to the daughters who aren't afraid to lose money for peace of mind
Shout out the woman who called out that federal agency on Security Boulevard for not putting a stop to the workplace harassment and abuse in time

For allowing that sort of disability discrimination and abuse to thrive
Like our mothers fail to believe our reporting each time
And just like her, that agency on that boulevard named Security refuses to see the light.

26

When there is no acknowledgment and no apology
The mother must take accountability
Otherwise it can never be
Especially when your mother is old enough to know better but lives in emotional and psychological immaturity
And that's why that type of mother-daughter relationship for many adult daughters can never be
Because of the resentment, dishonesty, and maternal animosity
Can't call yourself a mother when an evil witch is all we have ever seen
Birthing us and caring about us are two different things
Merely just having a daughter doesn't make you a mother to me
Only her Terracotta Warriors hold her in that esteem
My mother "raised" her sons but she sure as hell didn't "raise" me
She was my Critic-In-Chief
That was the only thing of significance that she taught me
In every card I ever wrote to her I was lying
Wrongly thinking that if I commended her for shit she never did she'd start trying.

27

The financial burden
Leaves daughters hurtin'
Read Soledad O'Brien's 2013 article entitled, "Mothers Who Drag Their Daughters Down"
And you'll see me
Adult daughters working to earn our pennies
But financially held down by our mothers tremendously

The parentification cycle rotates continually
And for her rent, bills and obligations we assume financial
responsibility for paying
When she ain't even deserving
And she's always hates it when it is MY money and on
someone other than her
I'M spending
Because she lives in greed and envy and she wants to be the
only one from me stealing
It may not be happy,
But I gave our relationship the necessary ending.


## 28

Distance is necessary
In order for me to be a better me
It is too difficult walking in truth and sincerity
When you have an oppressive mother in close proximity
Who is relishing in and cherishing her own dishonesty.

I know it is hard to ignore her lying and control tactics
When it comes to lunacy, she's mastered it
She's the type of mother who loves causing static
Then acting like she had nothing to do with it
Every word out of her mouth defies credibility and logic
I guess it is possible to simultaneously pray and practice black
magic
She and I are a horrible dynamic
She's so overly dishonest and dramatic
No daughter in her right mind could handle it
So I write about it.

## 29

"Ding Dong the witch is dead!"

I keep hearing that famous line in my head
Because for me it meant the end of dread.

I told her that if she said ten things out of the day
Nine I wouldn't believe
Because she's that dishonest you see
Her lies are like leaves on trees
And counting them all is an impossibility
The deceptions are far too many
And where the truth may be hiding we never see it clearly.

Think of all the things that she tried to stop you from doing
Remember all of the happiness that she tried to stop you from
pursuing?
Your independence and gaiety she was dedicated to ruining
All along knowing exactly what she was doing.

Why in the hell do you need her permission?
It's your decision!
She has always been your unnecessary pause and
intermission
And like a cat she leaves you defenseless and intentionally
agitates you into hissin'
Always criticizing, passing judgment, and dissin'
Ignore whatever negative comments she may have about who
you're loving or kissin'
And whatever your greatest joy she'll start destroyin'
Under x-ray her your backbone is missin'
Why do you even listen?

30

It doesn't matter if you're sincerely happy
She will let you know why you shouldn't be

Your mother said it to you and my mother said to me
So I decided to finally stop listening
Unable to believe the foolishness I was witnessing
I had to end all communicating
She had that much toxicity
In me she pollinates pure stress and anxiety
I am now willing and dedicated to fighting for me!
Stress and MS are mortal enemies
Yet, she wouldn't stop hounding and poking at me
To be around her is to live uncomfortably
It's very, very trying
What she tried to make me, I had the courage not to be
I somehow managed to break free
Even while her Terracotta Warriors were plotting and saying
whatever to recapture me
I fell for nothing
Unlike her, I wasn't destined to be a calamity
I allowed my mother to do what I wouldn't allow any man to
repeatedly do to me
She pretends so casually
Like a daughter doesn't know and doesn't see
That kind of "submission" always seemed abusive to me
Too much I was always internally negotiating
A daughter, a good mother should be protecting and
defending
But that never happened to me.

And my healing only came once I removed myself from that
crazy-ass family
And I stopped pretending like what was happening was
genuine and somewhat loving
Living within her delusional and critical life just wasn't for me
She wanted her daughter to be her partner and supporter in
assured misery
But from her mental derangement and cruelty I am now free
From her and anyone oppressing
To think that a mother would do that to her very own daughter
is surely depressing
Not to mention disgusting
But from the truth of it all there is no more hiding or ducking

Every family rule I'm merrily bucking
I'm no Terracotta Warrior, honey!
From her nipple that long expired milk I stopped sucking.

While she continues to live dishonestly, I'm creating my
destiny
There is no puppet master any longer in my skies condemning
and bullying me
There are no mother-on-daughter crimes controlling or hurting
me
She has a problem with strong women and she
only *truly* loves the ones that are weak
Take an inventory
The ones that are like her… codependent, unhealed, and
needy
Just like my daddy
She wrongly thinks that her faux-godliness removes her from
her ethical and moral responsibilities
And she will always refuse to accept any accountability
Really.
And she's only gotten worst over the years because her
minions let her be
She still is allowed to live in dishonesty
And debts that she owes I ain't paying
My money I'm not obligating…for nothing!
I'm happy!
And I'm proud of myself for fighting
And for not willingly crawling into the fresh hole she dug for
me
This daughter has survived her malicious maternal depravity
And now on to my female boss at work who keeps calling
The boundaries I erect she keeps crossing
I said to stop but she keeps going
Requires me to work overtime all the time but is never paying
I'm on vacation and this bitch keeps emailing
I'm on vacation so her constant calling I'm ignoring
So my husband she keeps calling
Electronically stalking
Now, a new abusive witch I gotta start battling
It's never-ending.

It's difficult being the only one willing to call her insanity out
But common sense to us, she still can't seem to figure out
The adult daughters of crazy-ass mothers know exactly what
I'm talking about
I can just look into their eyes and see a daughter's hurting
Jill Scott's *Hate On Me* reflects our mother-daughter
relationship perfectly
While Jill Scott's song *My Petition* immaculately articulates
how she treats me
And Jill Scott's *Fools Gold* flawlessly speaks for me
I guess shady men and bad mothers have unique similarities
They have similar chemistries
Neither can be trusted I'm learning
But when Jill's music speaks to me
My own horrors and not necessarily that specific experience
am I'm hearing
To Yuna's *Live Your Life*, start listening.

<u>32</u>

Please understand that sometimes when daughters judge and
criticize other women like that
It's because sometimes our own mothers mistreat us exactly
like that
"I don't get along with other women"
How many times have you heard a daughter of an eff'ed up
mother say that?
So the innocent bystanders some angry daughters attack
Sometimes daughters like us just spontaneously snap
Things can get scary real fast when we are forced to react
And we can accidently fall into our own traps
Our own mothers constantly provoke us and antagonize us
like that
And any insecurity we are hiding
She meanly draws attention to that
But sincere and honest mothers of goodwill never to do that

And instead of her advances and accomplishments our
mothers talk about everything irrelevant
Daughters focus on mistakes and body fat
We cruelly discuss dumb and insignificant personal decisions
that have absolutely nothing to do with actually that
We often place upon you what we personally lack
Because whole and well-treated daughters typically don't do
that
They don't feel the need to disrespect that
They have much more confidence and tact
And leading the critical army there is often a mother leading
the attack
It's her mother
Daddy issues ain't got a damn thing to do with that
Don't believe that
It's hard for a man to stay when it's the mother that's all bad.

## 33

A mother's Narcissistic Personality Disorder often makes
daughters targets
A bull's-eye is on our chests and with our own blood she
marks it
She's the *Misstra Know It All* Stevie Wonder sings about
No doubt about it.

## 34

As a child
That crap should have never been present
But it was
And now you want your own daughter to relive it
You're sick
You're not a mother
You're an evil witch
And your heavy load we will no longer carry it.

## 35

From Cosby to R. Kelly

Why do we make child molesters and sex offenders and serial
rapists deities?
And make sexually abused girls the liars and enemies?
A self-assured woman amongst male siblings
Like me
And you gotta sit through conversations where the men in the
family
Either defend or seem to be on the fence about R. Kelly
Did he or didn't he?
Just listening to the victim blaming and denying is disturbing
I tried giving the women around a warning
The Catholic Church was believing
But why not them?
The logic I'm not seeing
I'm not understanding
It's crazy
Folks equate television shows and albums and movies to
practically raising the dead or something
And that's disturbing
Lordy!
My father, I mean, R. Kelly reminds me of Roman Polanski
and Woody Allen greatly
And none are we patronizing!
And my husband sees it exactly like me
And those who make excuses for their behavior I look at
skeptically
And then I pass them an application because they should be
working on that street called Security
For that abusive federal agency.

36

Two different mothers and two totally different experiences
and families.
Yet, you are me
I became a daughter-activist to help other daughters in
bondage get free
I had to stop our inner tragedies
And the genocide of Black Cat Daughters I became committed
to addressing

I'd spot way to many dead daughters walking
To do nothing
Somebody had to say something!
I had to make my mother-daughter experiences and
heartaches account for something
Or I suffered for nothing and that's disconcerting
I couldn't just do nothing
And I couldn't take another day of that "but that's your mom"
talking
And every soul dismissing
I sent packing
And with her faux-innocence I got tired of people siding
And all alone against her mistreatment I've always been
fighting
And my lack of trust with practically everyone has always had
me disappearing
Inside there has always been a secret war with her that I've
been fighting
And the older I got the more the anger began raging
It took me 40 whole years to release my writings
And I promised myself that once I started publishing
I'd stop running.

## 37

The Bible says that if you allow that child to stumble, very
clearly
That it's better to have a millstone hung around your neck and
thrown into the deep sea
So I'm doing God's work the way that I see
Except I'm not doing any drownings
I leave the mean ones breathing
See, I'm showing the mothers who set us up…mercy.

## 38

Just like the dope MC Nitty Scott spits it
Speaking what's significant
With the unafraid tenor of Killer Mike on The View
Out of nowhere I couldn't believe that I heard that man say it

With a plate in my hand I almost dropped it and broke it
"Young women are being bullied by their mothers and older
women"
Wait, did he just say that young women are being bullied by
their mothers and older women?
Well, I'll be damned!
Thank you Killer Mike saying it
For validating it
Sometimes we feel that even with optic neuritis, we're the only
ones who see it
Who feel the energy from it
And with the honesty of singer Tori Kelly singing *Funny*, the
truth I can always hear it
So I write it
Because I can feel it
And Foreign Exchange's *Face In The Reflection* helps take my
mind off it
When your family treats you like shit
And your mother is just that toxic
And you don't know how much longer you can handle it
Listening to those who get it always clams me a bit
Especially when I am highly agitated
You would have thought that I grew up in M. Night
Shyamalan's *The Village*
Music and Stephen King always find ways to take me out of it
Between his many works and me the energy has always been
all-consuming and kinetic
I'll forever be grateful to Tabitha King for reaching in the trash
and retrieving it
Because it wasn't until I was introduced to Carrie White's
mother
That I knew for certain that varying degrees of others existed.

I used to secretly call that house Castle Rock because you
could always expect a horror film scene
Music and King
It got me through everything
So when she'd act like I owe her for everything
I used to remind myself quietly
Internally

That normal and kind mothers do those same things because
they are kind and loving
And they're never charging
And what's forced in her they are doing it naturally
Because they enjoy mothering
So when I talk about my own raising
Remember DJ Quik, Stephen King, Judy Bloom, and Beverly
Clearly in all honesty
And The Hughes Brothers and Crenshaw on Sunday nights
truthfully
Because that's who you should be applauding
Because they taught me everything
Back child support to them somebody is owing.

39

Away from her sadistic nature she never wanted me to roam
And she NEVER supported me when I left even after all the
evidence was shown
And she even bought her Terracotta Warriors along
Husbands mixed with sons I call "hub-sons"
And you know she brought them along
They should be dressed like the Pips because they only sing
in the background parroting all of her songs
I'm on the bottom rung of the ladder Cicely L. Tyson tells
about
And the moment you are truthful you get kicked-out
I know what she's talking about.

They tried to force me to go along
But I let them all know that I am grown!
And over a decade letter he and I are still happy and our
relationship is even more strong
Every day we are proving my mother and her hub-sons wrong
Even when no one in my family supported me moving on
I still got gone!
And like Bettie Page said,
Christian fundamentalist always see divorce as the worst of
the wrongs
Well, I'm writing different music

As my faux-family keeps singing the ole' outdated same song.

### 40

What is a daughter to do?
When your mother doesn't love you
Doesn't even really like you
And you know it to be true
The family façade you've been wearing ain't you
The broken path she took she demands of you
How cruel?
Everything she has ever chosen I would not choose.

### 41

Daughters may your pain and heartache make you better and
not bitter
For those who must go
Know you are heroes
Perfection is a fallacy so never let her try to make you your
own dream killer
Stop crying
With you we are all standing.

### 42

She's toxic
Some mothers only teach daughters to be codependent
That's what mine did
In my home my husband and I co-rule
And when my strategies work she hate bearing witness to the
truth
Seeing me treated well she hates seeing it
Our happiness she hates acknowledging it
Because she believes that a woman should always be
beneath and under it
And any rights her husband alone should give it
So when she comes with that female submission bullshit I
can't hear it
She's sadistic

Trying to project and predict the worst upon me like some
vengeful mystic
That's why I don't tell her or her hub-sons shit!
And before The Black Cat Daughters and our supporters
No one other than me will read it

<u>43</u>

I have zero social media presence
When it comes to trusting people I am always hesitant
When it comes to people I don't know I'm pessimistic
By the time I was six
I'd already learned it
When you can't depend on your mother you learn never to
trust it
Don't ever trust it
Don't ever trust it
Don't ever trust it.

<u>44</u>

I represent the daughters
The women who have officially flipped-off their mothers
With trying to explain themselves they no longer bother
The daughters who now understand their fleeing fathers
We are now the awakened daughters
Who are finally looking under the restricted sheets and the
soiled covers
The girls who inherited the balls that were always missing
from their brothers
We understand and relate to the stories of one another
And we now recognize and confront the lies and the
calculated deceptions of our mothers
She still views herself as good mother
But we all view her as something completely foreign and
certainly other
To her daughter
She ain't no mother!

She pretends to be spiritually superior
A phony Christian who hides her interior
She blames everything on someone else or some mister
She gets acquitted every time and is never the sinner
She's a double agent who plots behind the scenes and then
acts unimpressed with her undeserved gifts around the tree in
December
Ensuring that her daughter isn't the winner
She's the most sinister
Always claiming that you are headed to the incinerator
But she is the master manipulator
She's the spirit killer
The constant agitator
Always pretending not to know better
And when it comes to your life, she acts as if she is the chief
administrator
When she is actually the maternal perpetrator
The pathetic human calculator
Yet, I am my own liberator
Always trying to control me
But I now say...never!


<u>45</u>

I know you're frustrated
She keeps getting away with it
But the reality is
She's just mad.

She's mad because you got it
When she refused to help you get it.

She's mad because you accomplished it
Even when she tried to stop it.

She's mad because you are happy and positive
When she loves to focuses on the negative.

She's mad because she could never walk away from a bad situation
But you exhibit the strength and courage to remove yourself from dysfunction without any hesitation.

She's mad and jealous because you got everything she wanted
When she didn't have the guts or the courage to go after it.

She's mad because you know it
Even though she refused to teach you it.

She's mad that you know how to tell the truth
Especially when lies are all that she ever spoke and used.

She's mad that you speak your mind
And she knows that you know how to perfectly circumvent and dismiss her kind.

She's mad because you didn't listen
You defied her when she tried to keep you subservient and only in the kitchen.

She's mad because you did it without her
You learn that you could do it without you're evil and bitter mother.

She's mad because everything she ever wanted to be - - you became it
So her goal now is to try to delegitimize it.

She's mad because her futile opinion doesn't matter
Her authorization and blessing you are no longer after.

She's mad because you can see all the way through it
You no longer believe that fake "you need family" bullshit.

She's mad because you accomplished it
Even when she was unsupportive and tried to impede it.

She's mad because you can no longer feel her wrath
You've made your own way and carved your own path.

She's jealous of the butt-cheek-length waves and curls in your
hair
You exude external confidence and inner beauty she could
never dare.

She's mad because you confronted and tackle the real issues
You bravely spoke your mind when she tried to discredit and
dismiss you.

She's mad because you didn't need her support
You rightfully ignored her criticalness, negativity, and
insensitive retorts.

She's mad because you refused to establish the type of family
that she wanted you to have
You did it your way and you are immensely glad.

She's mad because you won't buy any of her lame-ass
excuses
You trust your recollection and recall all of her calculating
dishonesties and abuses.

She's mad because you will not fill their pretty little heads with
the nonsense that she taught
You have taught other daughters to be brave and to know
when to walk.

She's mad because you were right and she got you all wrong
You trusted your intuition when she refused to go along.

She's mad because you decided to choose
When she tried to convince you differently, you were
unmoved.

She's mad because you two do for each other
There is no one person valued over the other.

She's mad because you are loyal
Her disloyalty and underhandedness in your relationship has taken its final toll.

She's mad because you do not believe her gospel
When your mother is a liar and deceiver, that's freakin' impossible!

She's mad because you know the truth
That she did it all for her own ego when she said that it was all for you.

She's mad because you are appropriately holding her responsible
You recognize that she's lying as she pretends like it's all deniable.

She's mad because you are the better woman
You never settled for the abuse or mistreatment of any woman or man.

She's mad because you foiled her plans
You became the admirable woman who decided to ignore her bullshit and took a stand.

She's mad because you know who you are
You learned to accept yourself without her feathers and tar.

She's mad because you are capable of fighting your own battles
You refused to live the life of a downtrodden woman restricted by generational shackles.

She's mad because you are smarter
You don't believe her untruths and you recognize your inner power as a steely daughter.

She's mad because she wasted her life
Happily living for you means no longer paying her price.

She's mad because you're not in church pretending all day like her
With her phony, self-serving, and oppressive doctrine, you refuse concur.

She's mad because you're internally beautiful
You learned that being sincere and honest on the inside is just as crucial.

She's mad because you are at peace
You have remained kind and loving even with that illness and disease.

She's mad because you had the heroism to change what you didn't like
You accomplished every goal despite her criticisms and angry words full of spite.

She's mad because you defended yourself when no one else would
You chose to utilize your experiences to help other adult daughters and do good.

She's mad because you make smarter financial decisions
While she and the Joneses are headed towards an overspending collusion.

She's mad because you created and cultivated the life that you have always wanted
And you didn't give up even when she moaned, complained, and grunted.

She's mad because you built a house of solitude and love that everyone dreams about
Not the childhood homes devoid of love, where are you couldn't wait to get out.

She's mad because you have a loving and supportive relationship

She's jealous of your ability to move past a youth that was
loveless and catastrophic.

She's mad because you won't take her shit
She acts like a 13<sup>th</sup> disciple, and when it comes to the Bible,
she apparently wrote it!

She's mad because your life is freakin' awesome and super
dope!
You say kindhearted things while she uses dogma to cope.

She's mad because you realized that she can't be trusted
For her real sincerity and honest concern you once lusted.

She's mad because you have an optimistic and inspiring
attitude
And you no longer tolerate her churchy vitriol and crystal-clear
attempts to be rude.

She's mad because you didn't let her beat you
She can no longer talk down to you and you will now decide
for yourself when it is through!

She is mad because you are seeking
You know what you deserve and you refuse to be a weakling.

She's mad because you won't just walk her crooked line
When it comes to her family drama and bullshit, you don't
have the time!

She's mad because you fought for what you wanted
And you got it because you demanded it.

She's mad because you live life on your own terms
And only through your courageous experiences could you truly
learn.

She's mad because you have that glow
The kind of luminesce that doesn't pass through the ultra-
critical and preachy people you know.

She's mad because you somehow obtained it anyway
Even when she tried to block you and deliberately get in your way.

She's mad because your life turned out better
Instead of being supportive, she morphed into your hater.

She's mad because you don't need her for shit
And you didn't have to lie or cheat or mistreat anyone to get it!

She's mad because you see through her
You know that her phony sainthood act sets a low bar.

She's mad because you know that she's a liar
And all of her cruel directives and marching orders are officially retired!

She's mad because you are content
Yet, she searches for any opportunity to inform you of a newly broken commandment.

She's mad because you successfully played by your own rules
And to her, you have absolutely NOTHING to prove!

She's mad because you have true compassion
Despite all of her judgment and cruel reactions.

She's mad because you overcame
You learned that there was no safety or truth housed under her name.

She's mad because you looked beyond her church pew
You learned to advantageously separate them from you.

She's mad that you finally the hyperpigmentation and troubled skin that plagued you your whole life
And you forgave her for what she did to your face just six days before your photo from junior high.

She's mad because she can't take the credit
It is not okay for her to claim ownership or involvement in
anything that you work for and rightfully demanded.

She's mad because without her you still managed
You moved far away from her and them, to further minimize
the damage.

She's mad because you adore your children and she dislikes
you
She knows it's true.

She's mad because you aren't codependent
Remember when she tried to convince you that married
women shouldn't be independent?

She's mad because you will not allow yourself to be
disrespected
You know that her wicked secrets and true nature can no
longer be protected.

She's mad because her bad behavior and pious criticisms are
no tolerated
Your mother plays the victim when she is the one who
instigated it!

She's mad because she is no longer allowed in your home
You finally realized where her negative energy and
disapproving attitude will NOT belong!

She's mad because you spoke truth to power
You told her how you felt and you did not cower.

She's mad because you confronted the discrimination in your
federal workspace
When she tried to discourage you to keep you in your place.

She's mad because you got away
You made a run for it when she tried to make you stay.

She's mad because you created a different type of family
You realize that what you saw and hated didn't have to be.

She's mad because you redefined womanhood
You are the type of woman that your mother and grandmother
never quite understood.

She's mad because you are calm
You have bravely battled and endured a lot, but you never
rang the alarm.

She's mad because you know what you are capable of
You know that it's not going to fall out of the sky or float on the
wings of a dove.

She's mad because you had the determination and strength to
stand all alone
You did it all by yourself, and proved to everyone that you
were wiser and grown.

She's mad because you won't save her from herself
She better pray that the money miraculously ends up on the
shelf.

She's mad because you are playing the hand that you were
dealt
You are happy being you when she wants you to be
somebody else.

She's mad because she cannot frighten you any more
She tries to instill fear and doubt, but you have bravery galore.

She's mad because you can do it too
But you do it because you want to, not because you have to.

She's mad because you refuse to submit
As she knows how you feel about all that ecclesiastical
submission bullshit!

She's mad because you have no problem saying what needs to be said
You focus on life and she's obsessed with afterlife of the dead.

She's mad because you aren't anything like her and you hate her family
And who they are, you will never pretend to be.

She's mad because you are not ashamed
Not everything goes away just because it's in Jesus' name.

She's mad because you succeeded
Her bad unsolicited advice, you never heeded.

She's mad because you did the very opposite
And now you are happy, so she's knocking it.

She's mad because you've proven that she isn't the mother she pretends to be
You didn't allow her to dampen your spirit or diminish your esteem.

She's mad because you adore and have the love of your life
You built an amazing relationship despite witnessing all of their dysfunction, abuse and strife.

She's mad because you don't have any sense of phony obligation
You have made it clear that you are only responsible for you and yours and your own personal situation.

She's mad because it is not all about her
You could care less about what she says, does, or even infers.

She's mad because what you said you meant
You did what was necessary for you and your happiness no matter how drastic.

She's mad because you are responsible

Even though all you ever heard was the deranged rants of the theological.

She's mad because you had the audacity
To live your life and to refuse to be her pathetic property.

She's mad because you never seek her approval or opinion
You don't care anything about what she's thinkin'!

She's mad because she knows that you know that she's envious
She's so jealous of her daughter's success that it makes her delirious.

She's mad because you made the right call
You persevered when she predicted your fall.

She's mad because you are not afraid to say it
If it needs to be said, you will not delay it.

She's mad because you won't worship her fake piety
As she lies and cheats and pretends to be some type of noble deity.

She's mad because you live in reality
She's the most miserable and unhappy person you know, but is always yelling that annoying religiosity.

She's mad because you are the carrier of a special light
She will never have your back and she will never do what is right.

She's mad because you won't lie
She's the type of mother that refuses to give any honest and truthful reply.

She's mad because you won't give her credit for just birthing you
Apparently she thinks that that's all mothers should do.

She's mad because you refuse to deal with her and her crazy-ass family
You are a badass and you refuse to allow ANYONE to make you unhappy.

She's mad because you avoid any contact with the stress inducers
Of your life, you are the sole director and producer.

She's mad because what anyone says doesn't matter to you
Her two-cents and their grumblings will not dictate what you will or won't do.

She's mad because you already know what she is up to
Time and time again, her untrustworthiness has been proved.

She's mad because you don't care about keeping up appearances
To you not even a faux-family funeral or predicament is that serious!

She's mad because she thought that you'd always put up with her antics and deception
She never thought that your dismissal of her would ever be your reaction.

She's mad because you value your happiness and your stress-reduced life
Negative reactions in you she works overtime to entice.

She's mad because she is not allowed to disrespect you, your husband, your relationships, or even your pets
Any attempts made by her to unfairly condemn you, you will urgently reject.

She's mad because you care more about yourself than you do her
Any claims made in an attempt to take credit for your achievements and aptitude is absurd.

She's mad because you ignore her crazy ideologies and
refuse to listen to her religious mumbo-jumbo
You know who she pretends to be, but her true self, not even
she knows.

She's mad because you figured it all out
Yet, she acts like you're the crazy one, and she deceitfully
professes not to know what your departure is all about.

She's mad because you didn't make the same repeated
mistakes that she did
You took responsibility for your mistakes and you realized that
her bullshit you needed to get rid.

She's mad because you don't live a life of condemnation and
jealous regret
She's stagnant and you are successfully embracing life and
mastering each and every imperative step.

She's mad because you refuse to believe her and her
brainwashed Terracotta Warriors
And you told her to her face that she lies and you don't trust
her.

She's mad because you didn't believe any of the sexism she
taught
None of the antifeminist and chauvinistic stuff she tried to
instill in me was bought.

She's mad because you didn't keep the family secrets
You acknowledged the truth even if she and your faux-family
refuse to see it.

She's mad because you married an awesome man and you
trusted your instincts
You fought for your happiness and rebuilt what she wanted
extinct.

She's mad because you have no problem cutting someone off

You have learned that ANY hindrance to your happiness and success must be urgently tossed.

She's mad because you are your primary priority
Her viewpoint and complaints receive absolutely no seniority.

She's mad because she has lost the right to criticize, insult and emotionally abuse you anymore
You acquired the ability to promptly show her and her negative attitude to the front door.

She's mad because you do not have her orthodox false sense of obligation
You do what is right for you and your household despite anyone else's situation.

She's mad because you do not have a desire to impress others
You decided long ago not to invest is the façade and phoniness celebrated by your mother.

She's mad because she is envious of how you do things
You do it your way no matter how much she moans and complains.

She's mad because you don't live in La-La land
And unlike her, your head isn't buried in the sand.

She's mad because you and your husband have worked towards financial stability
And she's always been economically dishonest and a complete financial liability.

She's mad because your family isn't comprised of any relatives
You refuse to surround yourself with the disingenuous and purposely negative.

She's mad because you don't believe anything that comes out of her mouth

If she exclaims that it is north you know to go south.

She's mad because you stop making excuses for her bad behavior
Nothing is ever about you since you aren't her church or Savior.

She's mad because you will not be bossed
Anyone dissuading you is obligated to get lost!

She's mad because you are fearless
And you cannot be discouraged or intimidated by her phony concern which reminds you of *Mommy Dearest*.

She's mad because you know that she is lying
You know what she did, but she's not worth all the damn crying.

She is mad because she is not allowed to tell you how to live your life
You know the truth and her bullshit will no longer entice.

She's mad because you won't tell her anything or inform her concerning what happened
You've learned over the years not to waste your energy or precious oxygen.

She's mad because you left the madness and you never looked back
You defended your decisions and you stopped buying her crap.

She's mad because you have the right priorities
And you have absolutely no problem whatsoever enforcing your boundaries.

She's mad because you admit your shortcomings and recognize your faults
Even though deception and dishonesty is her automatic default.

She's mad because there will be no more holidays celebrated
with her in your home
Her ability to be a complete and unapologetic bitch, even on
special occasions, has surely been shown.

She's mad because the superficial and unimportant things that
she relishes mean absolutely nothing to you
And you refuse to allow her to govern what you will and will
not do.

She is mad because you embody self-acceptance
You realize that's taking yourself out of the equation is pure
negligence.

She's mad because you cut the umbilical cord
You are certain of what you saw, what you witnessed, and
what you heard.

She's mad because she continues to make some very bad
and poor decisions
And instead of taking responsibility for them, she justifies her
ridiculous choices by invoking religion.

You did exactly what she demanded that you not to do
But look at her and then look at you
I unquestionably see you as the better woman of the two

We are those daughters,
The girls with the mothers that only faltered.

We are those daughters.

We sit across the table a smile as you discuss your loving
duo,
Knowing that you would never be able to handle what we've
gone through.

We are those daughters.

We will gather together and contact each other on Mother's Day!
And we will honor our individual and collective strength and survival on that day and celebrate!
Mother's Day is for us to also proclaim
With or without kids we mothered ourselves, so that's also OUR holiday!

We are those daughters.

We work tirelessly over the years to try to please their demented egos,
Acceptance and obligation were not enough to keep us from letting go.

We are in those daughters.

The daughters that know that the particular concept of family and unconditional love is a farce,
We are used to being attacked and accustomed to them taking her side of course.

We are those daughters.

The daughters told that God was going to punish us, but never our evil and cruel mothers.

When comparing our mothers to Lucifer, we can't tell one derived from the other.

We are those daughters.

The daughters who refuse to attend the funerals,
We will not play the game of pseudo-grief and phoniness just to appease other people.

We are those daughters.

We are the daughters of mothers who are secretly jealous of us,

So it is always difficult for us to believe others and it is always arduous for us to trust.

We are those daughters.

We are the adult daughters constantly being criticized and judged,
And we would learn over the years that non-family is often safer than blood.

We are those daughters.

When other adult children discuss their mothers, they can't help but appreciate,
But when it comes to our mothers, we can never really relate.

We are those daughters.

We are the daughters determined to give our own daughters the love and acceptance that we never received,
And when our own daughters bare their souls to us, they will be believed.

We are those daughters.

We are the daughters who wished that our mothers treated us as good as the folks in the church,
Instead of loving and supporting us, we were always left in a lurch.

We are those daughters.

We are the daughters who were constantly devalued and mistreated,
No matter how we felt, or were treated, our mothers refused to acknowledge it or even accept it.

We are those daughters.

We are the daughters who learned to ignore our crazy-ass mothers,
And we gladly removed and detached ourselves from any blameworthy cousins, aunts, and brothers.

We are those daughters.

We are the daughters who did it own our own,
We ultimately decided to live a truthful life despite the dishonesty and meanness our mothers have always shown.

We are those daughters,
The ones who are far wiser than our mothers.

46

But we smile and pretend to be sociable while our soul covertly sulks.

There is no cure-all remedy for the daughter that's has always been misled,
When the father is horrific,
But the mother's deception and lies are twice as bad.

It's hard to tell which one is worst,
They collectively covered it all up,
Therefore, both deserve to be equally rebuked and cursed.

It is so painful and difficult to come to terms with,
Like you, I too had to admit it,
The mother is far worst in comparison,
And is far more sadistic,
That type of emotional abuse
I will never, ever, ever miss it.
I finally realized.

47

Sometimes mothers dishearten their daughters

Sometimes mothers never tell their daughters that they are beautiful
Sometimes mothers plot against their very own daughters
Sometimes mothers destroy the spirit of their daughters
Sometimes mothers clip the wings of their daughters
Sometimes the word "mother" means to suffer
Sometimes mothers never really appreciate their daughters
Sometimes jealous mothers emotionally abuse their daughters
Sometimes mothers covet the tenacity and determination of their daughters
Sometimes mothers try to squash the will within their daughters
Sometimes mothers fail to teach their daughters any meaningful life skills

Sometimes mothers think that a roof and food are the only things required to be a mother
Sometimes mothers try to control their daughters even as adults
Sometimes mothers only offer faux-love when they are in control of the daughter
Sometimes mothers try to make their daughters subservient to others
Sometimes mothers raise their daughters believing that it is permissible by God for a man to physically and emotionally abuse a woman

Sometimes mothers are dismissive of their daughters
Sometimes mothers cross sacred boundaries
Sometimes mothers violate the trust of their daughters
Sometimes mothers never apologize for mistreating their daughters
Sometimes mothers "apologize" but we can't rust it
Sometimes mothers continually lie to their daughters
Sometimes mothers value and worship the devious sons and belittle the daughters

Sometimes mothers are not who they pretend to be
Sometimes mothers hide the truth
Sometimes mothers sell out their daughters

Sometimes mothers refuse to meaningfully help their daughters
Sometimes mothers purposefully give bad advice to their daughters

Sometimes mothers disregard and discount the opinions of their daughters
Sometimes mothers knowingly fully steer their daughters in the wrong direction
Sometimes mothers refuse to support the good decisions of the daughter
Sometimes mothers fail to see their daughters as distinct and separate individuals

Sometimes mothers disrespect and dishonor her their daughters
Sometimes mothers do it for themselves and pretend that it is for the daughter
Sometimes mothers expect daughters to live the family lie
Sometimes mothers expect their daughters to live the life of the damned
Sometimes mothers expect daughters to live life as dishonorably as them

Sometimes mothers unfairly expect daughters to be as dishonest as them
Sometimes mothers wrongly blame the father in an attempt not to take ownership
Sometimes mothers pretend to be perfect
Sometimes mothers hate seeing our happiness and open affection with our love
Sometimes mothers slander and speak ill of their daughters
Sometimes mothers expect daughters to live their lives always trying to impress the evil and judgmental mother

Sometimes mothers expect daughters to keep up phony appearances
Sometimes mothers work to dismantle the confidence of the daughter

Sometimes mothers envy the daughters ability to make better decisions than them
Sometimes mothers expect to their daughters to keep all of the bullshit a secret
Sometimes mothers encourage the sons and discourage the daughters

Sometimes mothers think that it is all about them
Sometimes mothers only pretend to love their daughters in an attempt to use them
Sometimes mothers expect to be financially rescued by the daughter she mistreats
Sometimes mothers try to manipulate and confuse their daughters
Sometimes mothers orchestrate and conceal the abuse of the daughter

Sometimes mothers never protect, support, or defend their daughters
Sometimes mothers seek relationships with those who harm and abuse their daughters
Sometimes mothers pretend like they don't play a role in the dysfunction
Sometimes mothers pretend to be saintly, but they teach their daughters how to lie
Sometimes mothers try to use the Bible, dogma, and religion to suffocate and kill the spirits of the daughters

Sometimes mothers attempt to dampen the positive outlook of the daughters
Sometimes mothers relish in the medically unfortunate diagnosis of the daughter
Sometimes mothers are just sick and twisted individuals
Sometimes mothers lie so much that nothing that they say it is believable
Sometimes mothers are mentally disturbed and live in worlds that do not exist

Sometimes mothers are unsympathetic and have no empathy for their daughters

Sometimes mothers cannot be trusted or depended on
Sometimes mothers use unfortunate situations to exclaim a faux-spiritual superiority
Sometimes mothers refuse to adhere to the wishes and wants of the adult daughter
Sometimes mothers intentionally ignore the boundaries of the daughter

Sometimes mothers purposely and knowingly place their daughters in unhealthy positions
Sometimes mothers never work for the good of the daughter
Sometimes mothers try the place the generational curse of the family onto the daughter
Sometimes mothers only pretend to care about their daughters when they want something
Sometimes mothers never genuinely care for her daughters

Sometimes mothers work to make their daughters dependent and not independent
Sometimes mothers work to discredit honest daughters
Sometimes mothers erect Terra-Cotta Warriors to defend them from their wrongdoings
Sometimes mothers are mean, vicious, and evil to their daughters
Sometimes mothers secretly dislike and are envious of their daughters

Sometimes mothers strive to ensure that their daughters will live a life of misery
Sometimes mothers raise daughters to be subservient doormats to men
Sometimes mothers try to take credit for the excellence of the daughter
Sometimes mothers are compulsive liars
Sometimes mothers are narcissistic and nefarious

Sometimes mothers make it all about them when it should be all about the daughter
Sometimes mothers try to discredit the good decision-making of the daughter

Sometimes mothers resent the healthy and loving relationships of the daughter

Sometimes mothers intentionally direct daughters in the wrong direction

Sometimes mothers pretend to be innocent when they are surely guilty

Sometimes mothers pretend like they didn't see what the clearly daughter saw

Sometimes mothers emotionally, spiritually, and financially deplete their daughters

Sometimes mothers financially misuse and take financial advantage of their daughters

Sometimes mothers act as if their daughters owe them something

Sometimes mothers do not respect the right of the adult daughter to make her own decisions

Sometimes mothers try to manipulate and control daughters through spiritual abuse and fear

Sometimes mothers encourage daughters to stay in stifling and abusive relationships

Sometimes mothers take the side of the lying abuser over the daughter

Sometimes mothers never teach their daughter about healthy relationships

Sometimes mothers never support the goals and desires of the daughter

Sometimes mothers want their daughters to struggle and be unhappy

Some mothers secretly want their daughters to make bad decisions like they did

Sometimes mothers are too toxic to have a relationship with

Sometimes mothers religiously disrespect and purposely insult their daughters

Sometimes mothers wrongfully and willfully disrupt the relationship between fathers and daughters

Sometimes mothers see the daughters as opponents

Sometimes mothers only love conditionally and not
unconditionally
Sometimes mothers are jealous of the attention daughters
receive from their fathers
Sometimes mothers are the secret enemies of their daughters
Sometimes mothers believe that their daughters are worth
less and are not a valuable as their sons

Sometimes mothers only pretend love their daughters
Sometimes mothers never own up to what they did or what
they continue to do
Sometimes mothers are just plain psycho, crazy-ass, evil,
faux-religious bitches!

We are the motherless daughters
Sometimes daughters have to emotionally detach and get far,
far away
We know that her toxicity and narcissism will destroy us if we
stay
Her evil deeds, lies, and denial will consume us one day
We can't wait for tomorrow
We must remove ourselves today.


48

The Witchy Witch of the West!
She loves being your nemesis
While doubling as an Evangelist
But in your life, she always plays the witchy protagonist
The hidden and cruel antagonist.

She is a lost cause
Her trail of deception should rightfully give you pause.

49

Remember the day that it became unsalvageable?
When you could no longer ignore that deplorable
And in your heart you knew it was all highly possible

When the truth became nonnegotiable
When the cross around her neck made her idiotic excuses
even less credible
And nothing she says is relatable
If she spoke the truth just once, you'd have something tangible
But all the recycled the lies eventually became comical
A relationship with her it no longer manageable
Her need for regurgitating lies is insatiable.

## 50

Religion or no religion
It's your damn decision
You don't need her permission
To your heart and wisdom you must listen
Stop allowing her to perform emotional circumcisions
Trust your intuition
Make your own choices and make reaching your destiny your
mission
Stop allowing her controlling nature to cause you unnecessary
tension
A real mother would love you despite your beliefs and
decisions
And a real mother would not put in place specific love worthy
conditions
Live your life to your own selected precision
You don't have to subscribe to her oppression and female
submission
You are free
So why do you continue to live in her heartless and sadistic
prison?
Between you and yourself, she has managed to create a
powerful internal division.

## 51

You have been in a lifelong reform school
You will never matriculate and you will never be through.

You will have an insensitive dictator for a principal
There is only one book that you are ever allowed to read and
mark with a pencil.

There is only one narrow way to interpret everything
Yet she will claim to have the answers to every damn thing!

And there is only one perspective you are ever allowed to
believe
You will never, ever, ever graduate it now seems.

You will never be good enough to advance
You will never have a day off to enjoy a celebratory dance.

You will never go on vacation
You will never make it out of the school and there will never be
emancipation.

You aren't allowed to see things differently
And you will never pass her pop quizzes if you don't pretend
to agree wholeheartedly.

You will always be judged and scolded
You will always be punished work being a girl, but the males
are emboldened.

And menstruation and womanhood ensures countless hours
of relentless detentions
Where you are always wrong and she will always play the
victim.

She will never take responsibility for her bogus lesson plans
And don't expect a gold star for your good choices or for
surpassing any man.

You will never finish your assignments
You will never be the prize student.

You will never be validated
And the answer is never right if neither she nor the Bible said
it.

A girl is never able to prove herself enough
She will pound the ruler on knuckles and call it love.

You will never get a good grade on anything
No matter how much you study.

Expect to receive a failing grade for no reason
Never dare to ask her for any justification.

Do not expect any sympathy from her selected hall monitors
You will be forced to take the same religious courses over and
over and over.

And you will listen to the same tired and disproven lectures
day after day after day
You will have the same ridiculous teacher for life and she will
pretend like that insanity is okay.

You will never receive a passing grade
You will be fed lies and false information every single day.

You will be misled all of the time
Conformity is the only rule and a girl must dim her inner shine.

They may not believe you
But I surely do
It's time to choose you!

You are in her dungeon doom
Masquerading as an ethical and moral of school
She has everyone but you fooled.

Defect!
Start making your own damn rules!

Perfection is never a fair requirement
So, mistakes and all
I'm releasing it
I'm tired of it
I never want a book free of them
Errors?
I am them
I saw the mishaps and imperfections and I left then existing
To see if I could still stay standing
To see if I'd stop obsessing
So I'm releasing this series of books and I gave it my
blessings
The cure for perfectionism I'm testing
In me I feel the cure working.

## 52

You have nothing to be ashamed of
You have no reason to hide
I had to do the same thing
So I am on your side

It is hard seeing the truth when everyone else is blind
No matter how hard you search for sincerity you will never find
The individuals you are supposed to trust the most are never
really on your side
So I know how you feel
I too had to push them aside

With those that truly matter
I had to realign
For years and years, Lord knows how earnestly we tried!
For us to live
That relationship had to die

You are a courageous daughter
In that,
Have pride!

## 53

She lives only in the afterlife constructs of heaven and hell
When you have a mother like that
All current realities are merely just mere tales.

It is doubly hard when you are member of those communities
Where a daughter can't never freely admit that her mother is
the enemy

Where speaking your truth equates to blasphemy.

Since talking about the torturous mother-daughter relationship
prevented me from being heard
I stopped discussing it
And decided to speak through my poetic stanzas and written
words.

Deciding to terminate all contact with my mother was both sad
and exhilarating
And on that memorable and life altering New Year day
I gave myself permission to no longer allow her to be
debilitating.

As a daughter of both circumstance and genetics
What she thought no longer mattered
And I made it my mission to support and validate the
experiences of the daughters left tattered.

And my days have been glorious and more magnificent ever
sense
And for once, I granted myself full recompense.

And I decided to no longer come to her aid or defense
What I once thought was necessary, today I no longer miss.

Never listen to those unfairly describing your actions as
disrespect
It's all about self-preservation over of self-neglect.

Your faux family and shady friends may be on attack
But I want you to know that you did the appropriate thing
And I completely have your back!

No one means more to her then herself
Absolutely no one else
It's all about her, so for decades you've been sitting on the
dusty shelf
Catering to her embryonic whims before attending to yourself
She doesn't know how to reach for your hand, but she surely
knows how to grab the belt
Just the trauma and heartache of it all is proving bad for your
health
It upsets you to think of all the brutish and subtle cruelties she
has long dealt
That's why you left
You had to save yourself
She would have been your death.


## 54

She's always lecturing about forgiveness
But remember when she wasn't even talking to her own
sister?

She's so full of shit
But you have to act like you're okay with it.

She's such a hypocrite!
But you're asked to pretend like you don't see it.

They are as spineless as a wet noodle
Don't be afraid to declare what she continuously puts you
through.

Let them lie to themselves
But don't you lie to you.

## 55

If God lets you into heaven
I'm a shoo-in!

And don't bother trying to visit my mansion,
I ain't letting you in!

They say that all the people and animals you really loved will
be at the pearly gates
Well, then there's no real reason for you to even wait.

And as I walk down the streets paved with gold
If you see me please cross damn the road!

And with you I won't be sharing my milk and honey
You never repaid me any of that money!

In heaven what will you do?
There won't be anyone to judge or criticize or fool.

I will be in heaven too
I will finally be rewarded for all the years I've put up with you.

After years of being threatened with hell by you
I'd officially had enough.

In heave, I will be the one looking down on you for once
And you'll be the hot and thirsty one looking up.

## 56

The more she tortures your soul
The more you try to take hold
Standing up to her will required you to be bold
Disregard what they may say or what you have been told
It's time for you to work on being whole
Is time to disallow any more time to be stole
Peacefulness and freedom from ridicule should be your goal
You are getting way too old
Aren't you tired of never being sincerely commended, but
always giving her the undeserved gold?
The blood that runs through her veins is icy cold
You already know that she will never be able to fulfill that
maternal role
Her mislead advocates and Terracotta warriors either ignore
or clearly do not know
Nothing is real and everything is a phony show
Why have you allowed her to discourage you so?
I don't think your confidence can get any more low
This time you deal her the verbal blow
Hold her accountable
Make her responsible
Refuse to perpetuate her vicious cycle
Decide not to take it anymore
It's time to be bold.

## 57

She could eat twenty bowls of porridge

But will never have the courage
She uses words to criticize but never to encourage
I want you to know that you deserve it
You don't have to be perfect
Just know that you are worth it
You have already found what she couldn't
Distance yourself and finally put an end to it.

## 58

How can you allow that type of behavior to persist?
Why are you living in her land of no consequence?
As long as you emotionally and psychologically enlist
The uninterrupted bullshit will persist
She will continue to disrespect you if that's what you permit
But in MY house, I will not tolerate it!
If you give her a mile she will always takes way more than an inch
You try being nice and she still morph into an evil and judgmental witch!
But around others, she completely flips the switch!
I'm so, so over it!
A daughter can only take so much of it
Allowing her to disrespect you ensures that the aftermath will be verbally and emotionally catastrophic
She is a lunatic professing to be your mother
But she is nothing more than an everyday run-of-the mill type false prophet
Her behavior defies any logic.

Once you are this tired
You become bothered.

Just because she's lying
Doesn't me that you have to sit there smiling.

You are an adult now
You do not have to suffer through relationships that aren't
worth your while.

Obligated to remain on an oppressive team
Relatives also portray enemies it seems.

You are worthy, despite what she said
You are trying to seek acceptance from someone who is
emotionally dead.

For yourself only you are responsible
Thinking that you can change her is purely irrational.

At times you may feel alone
On those days take me along.

I too, tried to make right what was always wrong
You are not walking through this journey alone
The daughters will help you to be strong.

## 59

She smiles and puts on airs in the group,
Funny how she's always helpful and kind to everyone but you.

She's the type of mother who loves to expose,
So I don't tell her or them anything,
That way she can't reveal what she doesn't know.

She will judge me and criticize me at any time,
But the minute I stand up for myself,
I'm accused of being out of line!

She hates to see me shine,
Self –congratulatory smiling like she isn't responsible for any
crime,
She uses cryptic wording and every comment is oddly
sublime.

So I decided not to let her change my mind,
Everything that I ever wanted was on the line,
And in order to be happy,
I knew I couldn't let her inside.

By her rules I could no longer abide,
I have everything that I ever needed by my side,
And I learned how to be my own guide,
And most importantly,
I learned how to keep the she-devil on the outside.

### 60

She makes it hard for a girl to be self-reliant and dependent
My self-sufficiency strangely brought on her envy and
resentment
It is a difficult road for a daughter when your mother is always
your primary impediment
Wrongly raising me to believe that a working man was my
ticket to betterment
But I wasn't buying it!
I knew that I alone had the strength the courage and the
tenacity to get it

I knew that I could accomplish it
I knew that I could pursue it
I knew that I could do it
What she saw in me
Within herself she didn't
And you know what?
I got it!
I got everything I wanted!
I fought for it.
And I happily paid the price for it.
Because I refused to let her misery stop it.
That's why when I think of her
I never feel nostalgic.

### 61

You have given her a lifetime of chances
Now it's too late to make amends
She has never been someone on whom you could depend
I know it was difficult putting your mother-daughter relationship
to an end
She could never be a good mother towards you nor even a
friend
It must have been so difficult to constantly hear a hypocrite
sermonize about sin
And to this day, she gives the same sanctimonious lecture
again and again and again
It must have been so hard for you to watch her constantly
pretend
And then watch her take all the credit for you successfully
reaching the end
The pain of sitting across from that phony-ass grin

While she reminisces aloud about the days when you were thin.

62

When they believe that that's a part of you that needs "fixing"
Do yourself a favor
Stop clinging.

That goes for your mama too
Why are you so permissive?
She doesn't have the right to change or criticize you.

Even as an adult daughter you put yourself through it
If she can't respect you and your family
Open the front door and send her evil ass through it!

Do not allow your relatives or siblings to convince you
By saying, "that's just the way she is"
Her bad behavior isn't something you are NOT obligated to consent to.

Your house is your home
If she cannot respect your space, she needs to be gone
You're not in her house of horrors anymore
In your home you have the authoritative right to set the tone!

Everyone is afraid to upset her but you
You're a grown up now
She no longer gets to dictate what you say or do.

In my opinion she doesn't even get a vote
If she can't leave you be

That witch has gotta go!

## 63

You've put up with it for way too long
At some point you're going to have to move on
Life is about more than just getting along
The right is never going to happen when you keep bringing
around the wrong
You must learn to stand alone
To do what needs to be done in your life all on your own
Is to have the inner strength to read create a life vastly
different from what
Only then will you be strong
We are the daughters who finally stop dancing to her warped
song
With us you bravely belong.

## 64

Another phony photo around the Christmas tree
A Thanksgiving filled with spurious smiles and laughs
perfected for camouflaging.

When well it ever be actually real?
When Will I stop pretending to love people I can't even feel?

It's like a loveless arranged marriage
We go along with the expectations of others in an effort to hide
the damage.

We're stuck with each other because of genetics
But if I had it my way
Years ago I would've vanished!

At a certain point the pretending and phoniness became way too much for me
I purposely distanced myself and gladly flipped off anyone who disagreed.

For once I made it all about me
And I chose peace and happiness over who she wanted me to be.

I thought that handing out insincere love was what I was supposed to do
And I know that you are a daughter who thought that way too.

I forgive myself for not standing my ground sooner
I began to painfully realize, that as a woman, I was foolishly reared and guided to always be the damn loser.

I was habitually taught that what HE wanted was always above my happiness
And that as a girl, our sexist family system, destined me for sadness.

Adult daughters of crazy ass mothers
Forgive yourselves.

Forgive yourself for allowing her to bring her sexist and dogma toxicity into your life
Forgive yourself for always accommodating her and disregarding what you wanted and liked.

Forgive yourself for putting up with it for as long as you did

And for always giving her twisted opinions and oppressive ideas the highest bid.

Forgive yourself for making all of those excuses for her intolerable behavior
Forgive yourself for feeling obligated to emotionally and monetarily save her.

Forgive yourself for believing that phony-ass religious act
She is not mystically more superior or moral than you
And that's a freakin' fact!

But congratulate yourself too!
Because at some point you decided to do what you had to do.

You had the guts and bravery to finally walk the hell away!
You recognized that your family was poisonous and you could not stay

Even when no one supported you and her behavior they all would okay
You did not sway!

You may have wasted 40 years trying to impress your unsupportive and psycho-ass family
You refused to waste any more time unfairly suffering.

Congratulate yourself for living your own damn life!
That's not easy to do when your family is the lying and perpetually dishonest type.

Give yourself a pat on the back for having the wisdom to use your damn ovaries!

For declaring succinctly and verbally what everyone else
pretended not to see!

You are one bad and fearless bitch!
What generations could not manage to wreck
You superbly handled it.

Even when the scared and intimidated plainly hid behind their
balls
Your words were resolute when no one else would answer
that urgent call
It was the self-assertive and determined daughter who stood
alone and tall!

So I understand why you could no longer pretend
I too had to put the trauma and madness to an end
You are one of us now
An invincible and enlightened daughter and supported friend.

<u>65</u>

To be truly honorable
You must first honor yourself
Do not cower
It is time to be certain and prouder
Daughter, you are amazing
Declare it with guns blazing
Do not be ethically or morally lazy
You are not the one that's crazy
It is time to heal
You will be unable to illuminate what you will not reveal
Allow him to love you and hold your hand
In your presence, she is not allowed to criticize your man

And if she does
You need to take a definitive stand.

## 66

I decided not to let her make me feel bad about anything
anymore.
I am excited for what life has in store.
She encouraged me to seek a life of less when I deserved so
much more.
Her snide remarks and cruelty became harder and harder to
ignore.
The appeasing and week voice I once had now roars.
Every maternal roadblock that came my way, I kicked in the
door.
That pretending nonsense I now deplore.
And participating in the phoniness of my family has become to
big a chore.
I won't do it anymore.

## 67

For her forgiveness is difficult to grasp
Maybe it would be easier if the truth was known at last
But so much time has past
So many years spent wearing that mask
She pretends not to understand why you two clash
And pretends not to comprehend when you ask
You have learned not to walk barefoot on her road of
shattered glass
And you have learned not to respond to her verbal irritations
that itch like rash
She has placed shackles around your ankles

And she proudly brags about them being made of brass.

## 68

She is one that you can't trust,
But playing church on Sunday is always a must
You never find her peculiar and contradictory behavior
amusing
Especially not her constant faultfinding
The tales she spins makes *Sharknado* seem like a possibility
She has the exceptional ability to deceive while smiling
Just like my boss who is constantly boundary jumping
You say, "I'm off" or "please stop calling" and the phones just
keep right on ringing
And the emails to your personal account keep on coming
There is no break from the hounding
Early from your planned vacation you get bullied into returning
And well into the evening you are working but they say that
because of your disability And accommodation they won't be
compensating
Even when they expect you to keep working
And putting out fires those dumbasses kept making!
And those stupid asses put this disability discrimination in
writing!
And just like our mothers
The adults in power make bogus excuses for the mistreatment
and do nothing
What's clear to see they start ignoring.

## 69

The only thing missing from the story she just told are
unicorns

Guess I'm definitely a daughter scorned.

All of that shit was made up!
And these days, I just don't give a flying fuck!

Why are we all sitting here pretending like this shit is real?
Then I'm the disrespectful one when I tell the real deal!

Everything she just said is a proven lie!
And I'm just supposed to sit here and let that shit slide?

Not on my dime!
I'm not letting that crap fly!

All she needed was a dragon to authentic that lie
Because what she just said wades into fantasy story time.

This family is so full of shit!
I'm so tired of being the only one brave enough to say it!


## 70

She said that they are the type of family that never makes
provisions
And they keep making the same bad and destructive
decisions.

She is a daughter who is tired of explaining and defending
herself
She tired of softly living on the surface with a family that
refuses to go in depth.

She lives in a land of constant approval and judgment
With a mother who preaches heavenly prosperity, but can't
stay on a damn budget!

The constant conformity requirements are exhausting
Just thinking about it every night leaves her in the bed tossing.

She has lived long enough under a mother who foolishly
claims to know everything, but actually doesn't know anything!
So she's decided to covertly plot her exit strategy.

She can't move far enough away
And when she finds her new home
Her mother will not be permitted to stay.
There's no way.

71

The contradictions
The ambiguities
The hypocrisies
Have all become too much too bare
I have arrived at the point where I no longer care
At my watch I continue to stare
Wishing that I could be anywhere
Anywhere else but here
Even though she just got here
I am praying for the end to be near
The minute that she arrived I felt complete terror and fear
I try to be act joyous and full of cheer
Then I realized that I wouldn't take her and her issues into my
new year

I would no longer have to allow her negative energy to remain
here
I definitely needed that kick in the rear!
It was time to kick her negative and judgmental ass off the
peer!
In the corner of my eye I felt a single tear
Her little dig I pretended not to hear
And as we give each other fake farewell hugs that weren't
sincere
I already knew deep inside that the end of our relationship was
very near
Only the daughters like me understand why I never want her
here again.
They understand the situation all too clear.

## 72

I learned that it is okay to outgrow a parent
Especially when you are trying to grow and improve in life
And they are determined to remain stagnant.

My husband said that I give her too much power
So I thought I would feel better after a nice hot shower.

Why do I continue to give her so much of my energy?
Even though I know better, I still do it begrudgingly.

Negativity comes to mind what I think of her type of the
mothering
Her criticisms masked as faux-concerns is absolutely
smothering.
It is all just too bothering.

## 73

You are wonderful and good
Do not let her deceptive antics cause you to be misunderstood
Her behavior is personal, so we take it personally
When it comes to her dismissiveness and cruelty she is
definitely blasé
And her flippant attitude only conjures up more and more
animosity
I know it is frustrating
She doesn't care that it is you she is intentionally harming
Her disregard is both unfortunate and alarming
Feel free to do what you have been seriously contemplating
The banishment of her toxic nature from your life I too am
celebrating
Your love and patience is clearly not working
Freedom from her is just around the corner lurking
You have the right to stop the lies and the hurting
For her love and acceptance, you need to stop courting.

## 74

I have this burning and gargantuan desire in my soul
You and I have a daughter story that must be told
We have walked barefoot over the glass and the stony road
My desire to validate your mother-daughter experiences is my
primary goal
There is no need for idiotic outside interpretations or foolish
commentaries or polls
We both realized the danger in believing the lies and what we
were told
We didn't recognize very untruths when we were younger, but
we witnessed it we got old

There is an undeserved theatrical worship of our insane
mother that we just can't behold
And the truth of it all we can no longer hold
I know how you suffer, so I will tell them what your mother
wrongly cultivated and stole
I will poetically explain how truthfulness was something that
were never permitted to grasp or hold
Paralyzed by your traumatic fear of being unworthy and alone
Becoming aware of the lies and that deception, but afraid not
to go along
How easily we tend to revert back so what we were shown
Trying to keep her happy and pleased is all we've ever known
We know where her untruths are hidden and where she has
buried all of the broken bones
And anywhere that she is present never feels like a home
I will mention how hard it is for us to confront what was always
wrong
I will tell the world how hard and tirelessly we worked to be
strong
And how we worked against ourselves just so she'd let us in
and allow us to belong
I will tell them how her behavior and verbal abuse became too
problematic for us to any longer condone
I will also tell them how she was never a real mother to you
and how parenting was all wrong
And how we thought we could save a relationship that was
already gone
To her kind of abuse we were always prone
And how we had the courage to move past our fear of
rejection and carry on
We never wanted to believe that the handwriting on the wall
shown
For her maternal crimes she can never atone

Most adult daughters seem to put up with it for way too long
Our evil mothers continue their mistreatment and lies even
once we're grown
How many times have we pleaded to be left alone?
But her power over at us she no longer holds
We are now free to roam!

## 75

When your mother is your sure female rival
You are constantly fighting for survival

It is very, very difficult to live a life with someone always
plotting to bring you down
And when you look for a sympathizer within your own family
they are never found

Your whole life you are intimidated or bullied into going along
with the crowd
Hardly anyone believed you when you spoke the truth aloud

She will lie and deny responsibility in order to excuse or cover
what she has done
But celebrate in knowing that you are not the only one

You and I both know that every cruelty was and is intentional
It is impossible to move beyond the past hurts when you know
that her most recent actions were not accidental

You can disclose your grievances a zillion times
But don't be surprised when you are the only one courageous
enough to hold her accountable for her many maternal crimes!

## 76

You were born with an internal global positioning device
And every time you allow her to recalibrate your precise
system
You pay the ultimate price
When will you finally get it right?
You have your destination and goals in sight
But you won't use your insight
Her dark heart will never allow you to see the light
As long as you allow her to weigh you down
You will never take flight
It's not about what she permits or likes
You will never fly as long as she holds the strings to your kite.

## 77

What is mandatory for you is optional for her
You know that she lives
So why would you confer?
All of the dishonesty jumbled together creates a big blur
With only your truth as a woman should you concur
The destruction of the female child begins with the ma'am
Hardly ever the sir.

## 78

Let her be dumbfounded
You will no longer be her target.

Through emotional abuse she tries to make her wrong opinion
matter
But at some point you will have to mute her chatter.

She has a false sense of pride
The kind that we'll never permit her to apologize.

The kind of phony façade that will never give you credit for
being a right
Since anything other than a carbon copy of her isn't deemed
alright.

No matter how many years she's wasted promoting what is
wrong
Until the day she dies, that bullshit will remain her eternal
song.

You will never help her see the truth
Especially says she erroneously believes that the problem is
you.

She had to be amputated
She kept you're on heal wounds irritated

And she loved keeping you agitated
And with her removal, he unappreciative and ungrateful nature
is mitigated.

Her cruelty and cowardice is now officially abated
I join you in being elated.


<u>79</u>

Don't bite her bate!
This piece of advice you will learn to appreciate
She won't change no matter how long you wait

She will continue to spew out the same recycled bullshit that
you have come to hate
She will never own up to her cruelty or mistakes
She sadistically enjoys your emotional rape
Whatever joy you have, she will try to either demolish or take
While her Terracotta warriors and defenders sleep
Your eyes remain awake
Every casserole of misery and misfortune she will partake
But when serving cupcakes of happiness and joy
She refuses to eat from the plate
Understand that you are too late
You are a daughter who rebelled against her oppressive and
faux-maternal regime
A you declared that she wasn't who she pretended to be
It is okay if she can't relate
And if not going along is something she finds hard to take
In her fantasy life you do not have to willingly participate
Nor do you have to allow her to manipulate
Be sincerely happy it enjoy your life
She will forever imitate
Peace and security that you enjoy
She will try to castrate
You know that witch's game and she is never late!

80

How could we not have trust issues?
Especially when your own mother mistreats and lies to you
What is an adult daughter to do?
With a phony family and pretend friends, no one seems to be
honest or true
When you cannot trust your own mother, you just don't have a
clue

And your silence and complacency pardons what is wrongly
done to you
When we say nothing we are silently condoning the misuse
Despite what tiny morsel of truth we may uncover or produce
What's an adult daughter to honestly do?
When close to perfect isn't good enough to be considered or
approved
When your own disasters create in her a sadistic ruse
When others congratulate and compliment you, but your
mother isn't proud or amused
And for women with your kind of strength and bravery, she
has no use
She has a problem honoring a woman who is not under a
man's boot
Surely she looks like your mother
But daughters like us can be easily confused
All she honestly did was birth you
A mother isn't just something that you are
It is something that you do
That's why I've thoughtfully and courageously decided to be
motherless too.

81

I earned it!
And I'll never let my mother take me from it
I earned every gray hair on my head
I am proud of every natural silver highlight despite what she
said
I am grateful for every revelation and every spiritual
transformation
I learned to be proud of myself despite her cruelty and
indignations

I am proud of the life I have lived these 40 years on this earth
And I'm proud of myself for strengthening my self-worth
I am realizing my dreams and putting in the work
I am actively living the life that she made appear like a spectator's sport
I am living proof that a happy and peaceful life is nothing of her sort
I am the Henry VIII of my home and that she's not allowed in my court
She is not permitted in my castle
Neither she nor her atrocious cohorts.

## 82

If she were a boyfriend we would have long broke up
If she were a friend we would have long severed ties
If she were a job I would have alone quit
If she were just a relative I would have long avoided
If she were just a person I would have along disassociated
If she was my teacher I would have long switch classes
If she were just an opinion I would have long denounced
If she were a husband we would have a long divorced
If she were just a stranger I would have longed dismissed
But when your mother is your abuser
How does an adult daughter get out of this?

## 83

Stop being a chronic apologist
You have the right to live, breathe and exist
With that kind of mother the need to please always persist

You do not need her approval nor do you need her to take it
interest
Stop allowing that witch to be your protagonist!
I already know who irritates you, so cancel your appointment
with the allergist
When you have done nothing wrong avoid being her
propagandist
She is the one who should be the apologist
You don't owe her shit!
It's time for you to start acting like it.

## 84

Stop helping her to screw yourself over
Your mother is the problem stop looking for another.

Stop assisting her in ruining your life
You will likely learn that everything is different and better that
what she said it was like.

Stop I'm allowing her to instill fear
Listen for yourself and don't allow her to fallaciously interpret
wants you to hear.

Stop participating in the plots against you
Look beyond her recited Bible verses and be cognizant of
what she is exactly up to.

Stop allowing her to upset you
You know that what she cruelly declared is not true.

Stop holding your tongue

You have the right to assess your life and render your verdict
on all that she has said and done.

Stop believing the vacuous crap that comes out of her mouth
Lies and envy is obviously what she's all about.

She loves blaming everything on Satan
But anyone who fails to hold her fully responsible is
unquestionably deluded and mistaken.

## 85

It had to turn out this way
But I'm here to tell you that it's okay
Move beyond what happened yesterday
Stay fixated on today
You are on the dawn of a new day
For her sins no longer allow your soul to pay
Her world is black and white
Yours have specs of gray
I understand why do had to send her away
There was absolutely no other way.

## 86

I'm not going to try to convince you that I'm right
When you've already surmised I am wrong
Your games I will no longer play along
You do not have the power to weaken what I have made a
strong
And you are not authorized to shorten what I have made
wrong
I found strength in the delicate smell of my perfume
Why do you only find it in the scent of a man's cologne?

Once born, you have the right
To unapologetically live your life
The way that you want and in the manner you like.

You have the right to decide if you don't want to go that way
You have the privilege of deciding to think differently.

You do not have to regurgitate what you been told
Especially knowing that a large portion of the truth she
decided to purposely withhold.

I've learned that it is okay not to agree and to dissent
You can't think of feel however you want
And her criticisms you do not have to permit.

Generations and generations of girls being misled
Not by the men
But by their narrow-minded and ultra-religious mothers
instead.

Some say that gender equality requires both men and women
to rebuild trust
And although that is fine
A huge part of the problem lies with the backwards and sexist
mothers raising us.

I was raised in an environment where I was told that men are
somehow better than me
Where there was never a conversation about the hierarchal
dysfunction and preferences I would see.

So I decided, not to be her, but to just be me
The sad and pathetic life she planned for me I refused to
accept and let be.

## 88

She always the martyr
She makes me want to scream and holler
Faker then the currency bill reflecting three dollars
With her in the picture I know I'll never climb higher
Wow, I really despise that woman!
It's 103° outside
But with her it's always snowin'.
Where I'm headed she won't be goin'.
She's betting against me
But success and victory is all I'm ever showin'!
She ain't hardly knowin'!

## 89

No one understands
We've both been the unfortunate beneficiaries of her abuse
and demands
When you're freezing to death
She "kindly" offers her ice cold and bloodless hand
I will not allow her constant putdowns to fuck up my plans!
She's always been jealous of my inability to keep my head in
the sand
Any song I dislike she promptly requests of the band
Whenever she says I can't
I prove resoundingly that I will and I sure as hell CAN!

## 90

You did nothing wrong
You just merely decoded her secrets and you are aware of her phoniness
That's all
You did nothing wrong
They don't understand what it is like
To always have a negative and decrepit faux-mother always within sight
So, if you decide that she can't come along
Then that's alight
You will make it out of her sinister clutch tonight
No matter what she may say
Know that you are doing what is necessary and right
That uncertainty and fear below the surface she loves to ignite
She's a mother who is solely comprised of fear, negativity, and jealous spite
Retire from your sense of duty and your pointless need to be polite
More than anyone, I understand your righteous and worthy gripe
I too am a daughter of mother who is that type
I too was born into a generation of mothers who refused to get it right
But I've always known that their self-inflicted wounds would never be my plight
It's odd when your mother lives in darkness, but always preaches about a light
Daughters like us must always keep own happiness and solitude in sight
You and I have surely paid a hefty price
To have the opportunity to finally live our own damn lives
Know that our destiny and future is bright

Bid that evil sorceress an official farewell and a much-
deserved good night.

91

Let me just say it
You're wasting your time waiting for some apology you are
never going to get!
So I understand why it's difficult to get over it
She was wrong to ever cross a poet
A daughter with a gift will write and poetically expose the
narcissistic mother epidemic
She keeps doing the same evil and critical bullshit
And you're the only one strong and confident enough to call
her on it
Her cronies and Terracotta Warriors will always be pessimists
In her army, only the gullible and spineless enlist
Only the clueless and the shady participate in her trysts
And only the moronic would continue to put up with it
They somehow see an angel
But all you can see are imitation wings, a forged halo, and an
obvious witch!
She should have never crossed a poet!
A devious person can end up in a stanza before they know it.

92

Remember when she purposely locked you out?
So the evil could find you in roam about.
No matter how loud you would scream or how boisterous
you'd shout
She'd pretend to be oblivious and unsure of what the ruckus
was about
In church she has undeserved clout

But in her house of terror
You know what she's really all about
There will be no more emotional bouts
In your home
The villainous cannot roam freely about
Any door she goes in
You quickly and courageously go out.

## 93

She has a mother who is a psychopath
A master manipulator constantly warning of God's wrath.

She's never repentant nor does she have a conscience
And she'll the turn on you and betray you faster than Pontius
Pilate!

She wrongfully feels entitled
And is always tirelessly working to lessen your chances of
survival.

Before she even does it, you already know what she will say
and do
She's toxic and loveless
That bitch is trying to destroy you!

## 94

For me, there was only one way to feel safe
And that was to move far away
Significant distance is necessary for me to this very day
Phone calls and emails aren't even okay

And I refuse to modify my decisions based on what they may
say
It's my life
I'm finally doing this my way!

## 95

I have zero confidence in her ability to change
I guess she'll always be cruel and deranged
When a mother doesn't love or care for her daughter it makes
things awfully strange
And many don't understand how a daughter couldn't love her
the same
And for her intentional offenses she has ever taken the blame
When I think of a real mother I never mention her name
I'm a wonderful daughter to have too
What a shame.

## 96

Pardon my speech
But that witch is a leech!
Whatever you have she will choose to seek
She's your mother, but she's always prepared to compete
And since she can't win, she chooses to critique
She's already spent the money that won't arrive until next
week
And expects you to jump to her aid every time she blinks
What's the point in having a brain if you never manage to
actually think?
The repercussions of her financial dishonesty she's always
trying to avoid or beat
As the repossession man eyes her car on her street

With an overdrawn bank account she still swears she's elite
And pretends to be the most prestigious and holy every single day of the week
She's wearing you down and it is time to hit delete
She hasn't matured at all and the same madness she continues to repeat
Nothing she says is true
And you've proven that everything out of her mouth is a lie or obsolete
She treats you like an unnecessary appendage on HER damn anatomy
Always dragging you into her newest financial calamity
But the amputation of her was necessary and it just had to be
You had to detach from her neediness and constant negativity
You understood clearly what she refused to acknowledge or ever see
You did what you have to do
And that makes total sense to me
Daughter, she was dragging you down
There was no other way to break free
I understand
You're a lot like me
Feeling obligated to always conduct and organize her rescuing
I'm glad that you decided to no longer let that be you
And I'm overjoyed that the intimidated pushover is no longer me.

97

Money
That's what makes her happy
Her daughter's ability to make it
Made her feel like she had the maternal authorization to take it

Like her daughter somehow owed it
Any "love" the girl received, she'd learned to pay for it
If I hadn't lived through it
I wouldn't have believed it
Money, money, money
Take, take, take
I want, I want, I want,
Give me, give me, give me
Bigger, bigger, bigger
You better, you better, you better,
I should have, I should have, I should have
One day, one day, one day
I deserve, I deserve, I deserve
More, more, more
Deny, deny, deny
Lies, lies, lies
Obscure, obscure, obscure
Camouflage, camouflage, camouflage
Delusional, delusional, delusional
Critique, critique, critique
Judge, Judge, Judge
Hell, hell, hell
Fake smile, fake smile, fake smile
Pretend, pretend, pretend
The devil, the devil, the devil
Church, Church, Church
Enough to drive any sane daughter berserk
She doesn't care who she injures or hurts
I finally decided that she wasn't worth all of the discomfort,
pain, and constant work
But behind every accomplishment and success
I know that her ceaseless judgment and criticism secretly
lurks.

## 98

Let the daughters of evil mothers everywhere rejoice!
It's impossible stop a mistreated daughter with the truth, a
pen, and a voice

I know what it's like to be treated like the other woman
To have a mother so intimidated that she strategically keeps
you in the kitchen and near the oven

Constantly pretending to be so churchgoing
But the truth, honesty, and reality she is constantly ignoring

So I don't have any fond memories of what she considers
"home"
Especially since lies and untruths are all she ever reflected
and all I was ever shown.

## 99

Stop trying to understand the insane
She's your mother, but only in name
Over years of your life she took dominion and false claim
I'm proud of you for eradicating the lies she tried to house in
your trusting brain
I'm proud of you for courageously ending her brutal and bogus
reign
And for believing in yourself and your decisions when she
refused to do the same
Good for you for refusing to play her treacherous and
dishonest games
She's one evil, calculating, dishonest, and cruel bitch!
Know that you were never the one to blame.

## 100

The older I get the more she wants us to be alike
But the older I get, the more I realize that she just ain't right

My biggest fear has always been ending up like her
Constantly worried that she'd find a way to ruin and sabotage
what I worked hard for

After watching Discovery ID's, *Deadly Women,* I know the
mother I was assigned could have been much worse
But just because she complimented my wallet
Doesn't mean that I have to ignore the fact that she stole from
my purse
Pretending not to see the perceptible is something I am
unable to rehearse.

She loves making inexplicable plausible
She thinks that covering her ears and closing her eyes makes
it all deniable.

I decided that you and your family no longer matters
I replaced your cruelty and bitterness with happiness and
laughter.

## 101

Today, your hypocrisy doesn't matter
It's my own approval that I am now after.
When a man dotes on you and sees you as a little princess
Surprisingly a mother can quickly become the jealous
empress

When the love and accolades the daughter receives is what
she's always wanted
A vulnerable and trusting daughter can quickly become a
mother's target
When a daughter is unsafe among the men and even her own
mother
The daughter learns not to depend on anyone for protection or
cover
She learns to only trust herself
No other.


## 102

You're busy trying to show and prove
She considers your life hers and swears that her prayers are
somehow proof
You've already worked diligently through your daddy issues
Now it's your evil and narcissistic mother problems you are
laboring through
She's pretending like she had something to do with the
wisdom and tenacity in you
And we both know that shit ain't hardly true!
She has always advocated for the opposite of what you
wanted and desired to do
You meticulously repaired the tape on your heart with
industrial-strength glue
She's always fed you hot hair that was always impossible to
digest or chew
And who you are now, you always knew
She helped to block you, but somehow you managed to get
into
The God that she said disliked you

Helped you make it through
Don't let her take credit for your hard work and determination
Girlfriend, that's was ALL you!

103

She feels that she owes her mother everything
I am certain that I owe my mother nothing.

Her mother supports her at all that she does
But my mother never did and never was.
She told me that her mother hugged her all the time
Well, my mother did that too when attaining my money
became prime.

She says that her mother supports her and every decision that
she makes
But my mother has never supported me on anything not
derived from the credit she could take.

She said that her childhood home was constantly flourishing
with love, kindness and truth
But I don't recall any of the sort from my youth.

I've learned that just because a woman calls herself a mother
That don't make it true!

She mentioned that her mother only supports those who
wanted her daughter happy all along
But my mother only aligns herself with the men who've openly
done me wrong.

She says that her mother is her biggest cheerleader

But if there is a plot against me
My mother is typically the ringleader.

She says that her mother didn't have a weird aversion to discussing sex
But my mother has never had any conversation with me whatsoever about that.

She said that her mother is an honest and reliable realist
But my mother is both dishonest and emphatically capricious.

She told me that her mother has called her beautiful before
But I can't think of anything on me that my mother has ever said she adored.

She said that holidays with her mother are joyous and filled with love
I can't relate to any of the above.

She calls her mother her constant motivator
But I call my mother my unchanging agitator.

She said that her mother gave her constant encouragement invalidation
Mine gave me nothing but negativity, drama, and biblical condemnation.

She said that she could always trust her mother to bail her out of a tough situation
But my mother kept me stressed, and there was never time for solitude or relaxation.

She said that her mother was someone she admired

But I can't say the same since our matriarch was a devoted
and habitual liar

She says that her mother is thoughtful kind and considerate
But my mother is cruel, judgmental, and repetitively
inconsiderate.

She said that her mother has never broken or damaged her
spirit
My mother consistently did the opposite
That's why I had to put an end to it.

## 104

I am authorizing you to utilize my discomfort and pain
Use it to better yourself and your situation
Use it for your own healing and emotional gain
No two mothers are the exactly same
But ours are equally to blame
They should have been born with the same name
She's the faux- mother that actually never supported you and
never-ever came
Yet, you manage to still sing and dance in the rain
When she forbade you from driving, you were smart enough to
book the next plane
And when she tried to get in the way of that
You heroically got on the next train
She has no causes or reasons to complain
I share in your torment and dysfunctional pain
You are the type of daughter that any SENSIBLE mother
would be happy to claim
You are the type of intelligent woman that daughters
everywhere love to proclaim

All the praying in the world won't make that evil woman
change
How your head up high, girl!
Don't allow her to make you shame!

## 105

She refuses to even visualize and absorb me
I'm looking past her
While she's criticizing me
She isn't a decent representation of motherly
Nor should she be the poster child for love and humanity
I constantly replay in my head what she did to me
And how she acts like my truth wasn't likely
When was the first line I wonder?
When was the first time she compromised herself?
Not realizing that her actions would one day take her under?
When was the first time she stayed fearfully silent?
When her quiet permitted the wrong and reluctantly obliged it.
When did she give up on being a good mother to her
daughter?
Why didn't she put forth the necessary effort?
Why didn't she try harder?
It's difficult being a daughter
Of a loveless mother and a mentally disturbed father.

## 106

I know she's wrong on so many levels
Telling the truth doesn't make you some faux-family tattle
You merely dusted off what everyone could see on the mantle
She won't be relocating to an affordable apartment from her
make-believe castle

Accepting actuality for her is a losing battle
Getting her to see things for what they are is draining and it's
such a hassle
Once I put on my graduation hat and turn the tassel
I'm officially letting go.


<u>107</u>


She always has to be in control
Even your own self, you don't even own.

She only loves you when you do whatever it is that she wants
you to do
It's always all about her and it's never-ever about you.

She has narcissistic personality disorder
And your father is bipolar

You'll never receive the apology that is warranted and is in
order.

You finally decided to unapologetically live your authentic life
If anyone is not accepting and refuses to understand
Bye-bye!

I learned long ago never to envision my parents as heroes,
Whatever I trust them,
I end up with zero.

I've learn that it's okay to destroy every picture in the pile,
And to celebrate and I destroy every photo mirroring that
imitation infomercial smile.

I know it happened to you
When you realize that all of the lies that she repeated and
perpetuated
Were never actually true.

Even when you clearly married your father
She couldn't wait to deliver you to that sick alter
She rose the next morning smiling
Knowing all along that her daughter was destined for a life
crying

We need to set the bar from motherhood a little higher
Daughters look elsewhere when their mothers aren't the
appropriate suppliers
Yes, when it came to the be essentials my mother was a
reluctant buyer
So, if I said that she did anything more than the basics
Then I'd be a liar.


108

Around your family, telling the absolute truth is being impolite
Secrets are used to make things look glossy and appear nice
Everyone is expected to authenticate the family's faux-shine
But when you refuse to hide the grime
Your once stellar score falls to subprime
And your honesty is considered out of line
Because you spoke the concealed truth far too many times.

109

Depending on the gender they may not get it

To them the mother-daughter dynamic is insignificant
But to us, it's truly significant.

Any chance to reconcile or fix things she purposely blew it
Why should I protect her phony image?
I will no longer do it.

When you have a mother always begging and unjustifiably
demanding everything
You learn never ask for anything
You learn never trust anyone for nothing
A daughter often spends an exorbitant amount of time
contemplating running.

She's not the sole reason for you being
Her approval is not your reason for living
If she said it,
Always avoid believing.

She and I are no longer on-and-off again
I have decided to no longer allow her madness back in

She's the type of hypocrite that loves erroneously interpreting
what God would say
But now that I recognize that her judgmental and evil spirit is
no longer okay
I make the point to always head in the opposite way
I put up with her bullshit for 40 long years
I refuse to give that crazy-ass woman another damn day!

110

Other than looking alike
They are NOTHING alike

One has been pulling off a lifelong scheme
And the daughter knows that the truth isn't actually what it
seems.

The daughter believes that she can change things if only the
mother would try
But she knows that harmony is it likely since her mother won't
comply.

She's a daughter exhausted from always agreeing
Every word out of her mother's mouth excludes believing.

It's very difficult to strategize your life
When all you've ever received are no's, maybe's, and might's.

Always being there for "family" when they are down
But you are always left hanging and deserted when it's the
other way around.

When your "family" fails to FULLY and unapologetically have
your back
In the words of Hall and Oates,
"I can't go for that."

111

The honesty that the daughter welcomes
The mother is never seeing.

She always does it on purpose

And any defense you offer is intentionally misconstrued as
ferocious
But it is actually her behavior that is atrocious.

Through her antics, I think I figured it out
The advantage goes to the aware and insightful daughters
The ones that managed to get out.

Getting out as early as possible
That's the best route
Any daughter who has suffered like us,
Knows exactly what we're talking about.

Don't take too long to figure it out
Choose happiness
Her shenanigans don't reflect what life is really about.

It's okay to say it out loud
Despite her criticisms and judgment
Know that the daughters are proud.

## 112

Holier than the Dalai Lama
But it is always stirring up the drama
I gave her wrongdoing way too much attention.
I rethink and over-evaluate what I should have mentioned.
Then I wake-up the next morning and I'm facing indecision.
Chance assigned to me to her without my permission.
So, I have the right to write and its okay for you to listen.
I am a daughter on a mission.
Chosen to free the wounded adult daughters still in their
mothers' prison.

Living in her black and white world requires you to ignore your colorful internal prism.
It is quite difficult being the daughter of a hypocritical and judgmental faux-Christian.

### 113

You are not insignificant
And in no way is she somehow more magnificent
She's always been your biggest impediment
Ignoring yourself and what YOU want is completely negligent
You are a daughter charting a path where there is no precedent
Her cruel and discouraging words
Don't you ever believe it
In no way is your thinking or beliefs somehow deficient
With her mercilessness and meanness you've officially become impatient
No details shared with her shall any longer be intimate
Speak your truth and mean it
Don't allow her to revise it
Your history she'll try to rewrite it
She's lying
She remembers it
Don't concern yourself with how she'll take it
Your crown and scepter are waiting
You just have to grab it
Everything you've ever wanted is for the taking
There is no need whatsoever to apologize for the life you are bravely making
Don't stay seated when you need to rise
Your audacity and strength will surly surprise
Expect a few to roll their eyes

Her Terra-Cotta Warriors will surly sigh
And her enablers will pretend not to know why
There will be no more compromise
Your tongue will make them all realize
The lamented daughter is now alive
Make your shady mama recognize!
She's completely full of shit!
Daughter, you are the real prize
It's time to put an end to her deceptions and lies
The weakling is now the wise
You've finally opened your eyes.

## 114

All is not fine,
You have the right to speak your mind.

Once you say it out loud,
Know that you may lose what you THOUGHT you couldn't live
without.

You will live to see another beautiful day,
You won't die because they refuse to see it your way.

They don't have to agree,
They just need to stop obstructing your view so that you can
see.

You are right,
You never needed their okay.

Once you stand up to the devil,
All of her sympathizers quickly become less and less credible.

Do the impossible,
Your freedom from your toxic family is attainable.


## 115

It's so hard to get away
You try to break free
But they are always encouraging you to stay
To "keep the peace" they'll say
You are so tired of hearing that, "she's just that way"
Even as an adult daughter they still want you to obey
But that kind of cruel deceit isn't okay
Get out of your own way
If not yesterday
Then do it today
I call it toxicity
You call it your family.


## 116

There are those who help her get away with it
Everyone is aware
But you are the ONLY one willing to call her on her lies and
bullshit
She plays the same hand over and over
Always seeking to camouflage it
Yet, her bogusness you are somehow supposed to believe it
Any references or questioning about reality and honesty is
always off topic
Don't let your spineless and untrustworthy relatives separate
you from truth and logic
To them, honesty and integrity is piffling and microscopic

I am proud of you for no longer allowing it
Every historical revision becomes more and more tragic
Then you realize that genetics and misperceived duty alone
no longer holds any magic
You've finally disconnected from that damaging magnet
And even the bloodsucking maggots
No more fake smiles and waves like you are a daughter
competing in some bogus "Best Fake Family" pageant
Family deceptions and lies are like the sun
Burning off and evaporating spirits destined to be undone
Everything and everybody revolves around it
And over time, dishonesty and falsehoods always multiply and
become cosmic
It just sickens you to even be around it
Their lies will one day destroy them
So stay far, far away from it.
If they don't respect you enough to speak honestly recite the
truth
What's the real use?
Let them destroy themselves
But don't allow them to infect you.

## 117

Too scared to walk away
Too worried about what you're related haters will likely say
Why can't you make it about you today?
All those years you gave her each and every day
Taking care of your immature parents left you with little time to
play
God must have been busy that day
Because YOUR money was necessary to make their way
Calculating their expenditures as you lay

Why is you mother asking you?
To Jesus she better pray
That's who is supposed to save her from her self-designed
disaster anyway
Why is your wallet even in play?
You don't have to stay
Listen to me
Leaving is okay
I'll show you the way.

## 118

If a person doesn't respect you enough to be honest
They'll betray you
I promise.
If a person says that EVERYONE lies
But you don't
Just give them time.
They'll say they didn't say it when you rewind
Drop them
It's time.
Even mothers aren't immune
Beware of anyone trying to stop your bloom
Saying goodbye is never too soon.
Women today have choices
Daughters raise your voices
Be courageous
When you standup for yourself
Your bravery becomes contagious.

## 119

She's a lost cause.

Even her audacity to consistently lie gives me pause.
She has broken nearly every mother-daughter relationship clause.
You are justified to free yourself from her merciless jaws.
Free yourself from her vicious lies and gruesome "all about me" claws.
She will turn your heart and justifiable expectations into coleslaw.
It's time for you to lay down the law.
She's gone too far.


## 120

I've learned not to be afraid
No matter what my evil mother may say
I've found it more helpful to evaluate the beginning and not the end of my day
Being a faux-Christian mother with a vendetta against her daughter is not okay
I decided to do this my way
There is too much now at stake
I'm tired of sleepwalking through our relationship
I want to be awake.


## 121

Until I met you
I never knew
That a man like you really could be true
Someone who'd actually do all that he said he would do
Your truthfulness was something needed and refreshing to get used to
And all of your promises would actually be true

And all of your commitments you'd always see through
And to get to the actual truth
I never had to decipher a series of random circumstances and clues
I wouldn't be expected to buy a story that no liar could possibly prove
You are a kind, loving, and brilliant man who would remain personally, professionally, and educationally always on the move
Every obstacle you'd demolish just to prove
You were always determined to succeed regardless of who approved
And even though she never presumed
I always knew and assumed
You made it all come true
I'm so happy that I didn't allow her cynicism and criticisms keep me from you
I had no choice but to bid a mother like her adu
Her dismissal was something that I just had to finally do
I am unequivocally through.

## 122

A mother so vicious and cavalier
Transparently being a woman that the daughter knows is insincere
Has been living a lie for so long she thinks she's in the clear
But the daughter knows that nothing is as it appears
The daughter silently evaluates what she sees and hears
She would reflect on all of the secrets and deceptions she would witness overhear
Never the type of mother that a daughter should ever endear
But despite her ridicule

She will persevere
She refuses to listen to another lecture about judgment and religious fear
To her scriptural manipulations she'll no longer lend her ear
When she fantasizes about leaving her very being cheers
It's time to kick her college education plans in high gear
And when the coast is finally clear
And she no longer sees her ball and chain in the rear
Her momentous inner strength will lead her the hell up out of here!

123

Never under estimate the value of peace
It's necessary
To say the least
The drama that's in your family and circle
You will soon have to release
Especially if you want to end up in one piece
All of the madness and misinformation circulating you can't police
The squabbles and the toxicity will never cease
Don't waste your energy or time trying to change or fix what will never be
They always manage to get your temper boiling hotter than fish grease
Always worrying about your critical mother and what those fools think
But only YOU do YOU have to please
It's time to finally breath
Girl, take heed
Godspeed.

## 124

I'm always the sinner
She's always the saint
She's never held accountable
I own up to my mistakes
She's encourages unnecessary suffering and inaction
But for my happiness I will refuse to wait
She's always request more, more, more
I choose to remain grateful and just appreciate
I made it right
She's way too late
Protecting that phony legacy
I will no longer participate
She's an emotional terrorist
I won't negotiate
To protect my peace and sanity
I refuse to communicate.

## 125

The sons will become what the mother tolerates
And the daughter will likely mimic the behaviors the mother
emulates.

To survive in her mother's world she'd have to forcibly
assimilate
She'd have to pretend like she didn't hear it when her mother
would cruelly instigate.

Ask about the house and the mother can even recite the
square footage of the roof

But when it comes to loving, nurturing, and accepting her daughter
She can't seem to locate or recall that nonexistent proof.

So tragic
No wonder their relationship vanished like magic.

To continue living that lie
The adult daughter just couldn't manage it.

When it comes to that perceived genetic obligation
The adult daughter refuses any affiliation.

I think her father was a monster
And her mother taught her that it was permissible suffer
And just living made a girl child more susceptible and likely to struggle and suffer
The expectations are different when you are born the other
The unfairness and cruelty she suffered she put on another
And even on my scapegoat brother
I guess that's why she could never really be my mother
And that positive maternal absence just made me tougher
Now, I am stronger
The weakling no longer
I exceeded every goal and I even excelled farther
I rebuilt it all without the love and unwavering support of a loyal mother or father
I have all that I've ever wanted and all I've been searching for
I don't have to look any further
I am living proof that it CAN be successfully accomplished without a mother
But nothing is possible without the tenacious dedication and determination of you

The daughter.

## 126

Aren't you tired of being used?
Still dealing with the constant and repetitive emotional abuse?
Haven't the same old stories and excuses gotten old?
How could a mother purposely damage her own daughter's
soul?
Unless the truth is finally acknowledged and told
No one will ever really know.

## 127

It's so hard to be yourself
Especially since you spent so much of your life
Being someone else.

It's so hard being at the real you
Always doing it your family's way
Never truly doing what you want to do.

Too afraid of what they will think
Too frightened to embrace your need for solitude and silence
So you become the introverted girl who is always forced to
engage and speak.

Why are you still waiting?
Do you.
Any hapless existence is of our own making.

## 128

Heredity can be a traumatic life sentence
If you let it
It's so difficult to engage with the unrepentant
What she sees as a minor emotional inconvenience
To you it is quite significant
The entire episode is pertinent and relevant
Stop expecting a heartfelt apology from someone who will
never even admit it
It's over
To hell with it.

### 129

Your struggle and those tears were not wasted
Despite the odds
You made it
There was a story to be told
You said it
When you were being judged by her
You moved past it
When she lied
You denounced it.
When they tried to tell you to forget about it
You confronted it
When they told you to move on
You addressed it.
When the internal voices told you not to mention it
You still wrote it
To silence your inner critic
You divulged it
Daughters like us have an uncomfortable story
Most ignore it

We've been invisible for so long
Maybe now they'll see it
Being born with a vagina
Makes you easily susceptible to it.

## 130

Another necessary public service announcement
There is globally a problem with domestic violence
But when your emotional abuser is your mother
There is often dead silence
When we reflect back
We acknowledge that we never had the proper responsive
guidance
Going to school and excelling wasn't necessarily just for you
It fed the pious
And allowed her to take some type of ownership over the
miraculous
But over the years, we learned that our own lives aren't really
for us
Our accomplishments serve as a vessel for the societal
admiration that she lusts
So when her name is mentioned
They are always referencing a person we've learned not to
trust
So for us,
Remoteness is a critical must.

## 131

Because you are persistent
You aren't pessimistic
But your mother tries to make you hesitant

By interjecting language that isn't even relevant
She extinguishes your flame before it's even lit
When it comes to encouraging a positive sentiment
She'll have absolutely nothing to do with it.

## 132

Our roles have been clearly defined
I've decided to catapult forward and waste no additional time
I am the heroine in this grand life story of mine
My resolve and determination derived from the tears I once
cried
Every time I stood up for what I deserved, I gained a little bit
more pride
And her oppressive thinking and discriminatory
categorizations
I refused to any longer abide
And when their chaotic nature infringes on my solitude and
peace
I quickly cast them aside
Because when it comes to MY life
I freakin' decide!
When you have fought tirelessly to be the heroine
You have earned the right to ultimately decide
And if I like the individual
Maybe they can join me on this awesome ride!
I am a woman who refuses to hide
And I know that I have truth and honesty on my side
I'm wearing white today
But I ain't no virginal and delusional bride
And while those sexist mothers are encouraging and teaching
their girls to struggle
We are the daughters who will glide

We have emotionally surfed every difficult and sabotaging tide
I saved a cupcake for you today
With a birth control pill on the side
Prepared just the way you like.

## 133

I've learned the hard way
Don't believe everything your mother may say
It's likely happened a different way
Not everything goes away just because you pray
The mysteriousness of the universe and fate is often at play
The love was never truly there despite what she will say
Our internal investigations and emotional insights have
overturned every false claim
And the truth we will speak and no longer delay
We will thankfully never-ever be like our mothers
We refuse to go that unethical and wicked way.

## 134

One day you will tire from fighting her alone
You think that if you change the station she may sing a new
song
But you're dead wrong
In her mist is not where you belong
All of the scared men have run and headed home
They habitually turn timid while you become as notorious as Al
Capone
She'll scream at you and then hypocritically criticize you for
your tone
The lies and unbelievable stories she tells leaves your mind
blown

And her evil role in all of this she will never own
Therefore, her behavior only obscures what is really being shown
A faux-life manufactured under her illusionary dome
She claims to be all-knowing but you remain truly unknown
When she morphs into the bitch
Stop volunteering to be the bone
Relocate to a mood different zone
She's dug a pit for you so don't fall into the hole
Always make peacefulness and drama-free living the goal
If she cannot respect that
Just leave the sorceress alone
And be proud of yourself for not becoming her pathetic clone.

<u>135</u>

I know it's hard not to look back
Her Terracotta Warriors may excuse her behavior
But know that I have your back
Just stay mentally on track
Any display of cowardliness will surely spawn mean laughs
When you say your peace she will surely gasp
But your continued silence will allow the pain to last
And her horrible attitude receives an underserved pass
Your spirit has been stalled and she treats you like trash
It's time to acquire and utilize some vocalized gas
Or live forever in her delusional past
And forever wear that inauthentic mask
Stop putting your faux-family first and continuously placing yourself last.

<u>136</u>

A happy ending is impossible
When you are always under the scrutiny of the critical
Finding errors and faults are typical
She's the smartest one in the room and you're the imbecile
She finds swallowing your positivity and calm demeanor to be
most delectable
You closely observe the cruelty that she disguises to be
undetectable
The kindness that she pretends to have is untraceable .
You will never be good enough no matter how impeccable
So, just let it go
You we'll never have to convince me
I already know.

## 137

I learned it one day
Don't depend on anyone along the way
Never believe what most people say
Complete trust is never okay
Suspiciousness is a customary mainstay
With your very soul they will play
Constantly misled every single day
They are consistently causing you accomplishment delays
I know you're tired
Continuously being on display
It will be okay
Let's move past the chaos of yesterday
You will gain strength today
Don't absorb anything that she may say
You purposely disregard yourself
When you pay too much attention to the relentless critiques of
"they"

Don't allow that kind of cruelty to lead you astray
When they get in your waters
Transform into a damn stingray!
Stop trying to prove what is clearly obvious today
They'll pretend to be oblivious anyway
But it will all be okay
Stop being afraid to do it YOUR way
Their opinion doesn't matter anyway
They have absolutely no say
You have the unreserved right to be happy
And you have the right to distance yourself from those who
won't allow happiness to be.

## 138

Always living for the opulent
And can't afford it
Watching you constantly crave for what you can't afford is
tragic
Why do you obsess over the insignificant?
That house is out of your price range, but you still want it
The most expensive is always inappropriately your target
But that doesn't stop you from lusting after it
Now, the only way to get the money is to pray for it.
But that's some ridiculous and insane shit!
How is God responsible for you being financially irresponsible
and stupid?
Why'd you even purchase it?
You can't hold on to it
You KNEW that you couldn't afford it!
But you still got it
You still did it
Spending money that you don't have is just plain idiotic

That's why you always end up losing it
You knew from the jump that you couldn't afford it
But that doesn't stop you from wanting it
From purchasing it
As long as the people who don't matter see you as
magnificent
You'll pretend that the purchase was for some greater benefit
But I know you
And all of your justifications are irrelevant
When it comes to money mismanaging you own the patent
Your focus is always on obtaining material crap that isn't even
pertinent
Stop using the accumulation of worthless possessions to
make you feel worth it
Before you even get it
You spend it
To a nonsensical financial belief system you are clearly a
magnet
And all these decades later, you still don't get
Whatever may be necessary in the future, I guarantee that you
haven't prepared for it
And when it comes to repetitive poor financial decisions
Your horrid economic performances are notoriously chronic
The School of Common Sense is a free college
Please urgently gain some budgeting knowledge
Because I won't be bailing you out of it
So don't ever expect it.

139

It's too heavy to hold
Is time to just let that madness go
Stop trying to change an impossible situation

Stop trying to fix a mind that clearly needs some type of medication
And before getting involved
I strongly encourage you to employ a bit of hesitation
Don't allow your peace to be disturbed by their complication
Fixing that relationship can no longer be your motivation
Together we will get over her spiteful and hypocritical reaction
Don't allow her critiques to gain traction
It is what it is
That circumstance is unfixable
And her emotional abuse and judgment is always predictable
Anger and tears are always probable
But now you're knowledgeable
And you realize that you must break free from that dysfunctional cycle
And you realize that you are dealing with a complete psycho
You no longer care about being likable
And you don't care about being stripped of your unbearable family title
Especially sense your faux-family is comprised of backstabbers and rivals
Led by a matriarch determined to derail your happiness and survival
Girl, it's time to wash your hands
Rise
It's time to stand
It's your turn to make demands
You now know to disregard her ridiculous, faux-religious, and sexist commands
She can't walk all over you when you stand
No matter who decides to understands
Catapult you're plan
You aren't a little girl anymore

You've become a courageous and fearless grown-ass
WOMAN!
She's raised you to think that you can't
But we both know that you can!

140

She has a predictable reaction
And zero compassion
Genuine love for her daughter she is obviously lackin'
Offense after offense you are recallin'
She uses her Bible and religion to build your iniquitous
contraption
Insult after insult she is stackin'
She envies your motivation
And your unique ability to make a decision
Without seeking her approval and unnecessary permission
She can never just enjoy the cruise without being the captain
Her attempts to control you leave you perturbed and laughin'
Then you quickly see through what she is maskin'
Then you go in your own direction without askin'
Then your soul starts rejoicing and clappin'
That's how it always happens.

141

There are two sets of rules
One for the guys
And one sexist set for you
You're lip-synching through life
Just trying to be approved
But all that negativity
Impacts your joyous mood

With that constant convincing
You will never be through
There's only so much evidence producing one can do
Don't be surprised when they excuse what she aims to induce
You will be unfairly criticized no matter what you do
Beware of those pretending to support you
And those who think that changing your mind is necessary to
do
They very well may express doubts
But doubting and insecurity we don't do
I'm a woman who's been through it too
And your biggest haters can be relatives too
But know that I believe you
You aren't alone
I'm with you too
I'm writing this for you
We'll miraculously make it through
And we will obtain the freedom we are due
And we will be forever known as the courageous two
You for me
And me for you.

## 142

One day it just all became too much
I was tired of being ridiculed
And kicked consistently in the gut
I'd had enough
Being in that family became way too tough
The path could have been so much easier
But she labored diligently to brainwash me and make my
journey rough
To her demented way of thinking I felt cuffed

It became nonviable to hoard all that emotional stuff
I just got to the point where I'd had enough
All of the repetitive and vapid nonsense just became way too
much
As far as I'm concerned
They're all mentally out to lunch
I now live in peace and happiness
Here, I can't be touched
I love myself way too much
To continue to put up with such.

## 143

When you are the one who earned it
They can't take it
But I don't understand why you think that you can't make it?
Mothers often do daughters a disservice when they raise us to
expect it
When they intentionally infer that we can't solely earn or
achieve it
But listen to me, daughters
That kind of thinking will leave you stagnant
You don't have to put up with any disrespect just so you obtain
a portion of it
Never settle for a little bit
To accomplish greater you are already equipped
Her kind of thinking
I encourage you to decline it
Please don't believe it
That mindset
We must never enable it
We are the daughters who will expel it
If we don't infiltrate we can't pursue it

Watch her watch us do it!

## 144

To be unapologetically 40
I no longer need to prove to her that I am worthy
I survived a mother who constantly incites worry
She looks righteous,
But is actually demeaning and unholy
Always has a different excuse and farfetched story
For her
Honesty and truth are just too boring
And sincerity and integrity is way too gory
But I got out
Glory.

## 145

I have the memory of an elephant
I will never forget it.

She did the best that she could at the time
How many daughters are tired of hearing the same old
ridiculous line?

She didn't do her best
And to that I can attest.

I lived through her war zone during that time
That evil woman should be brought up on war crimes.

She didn't do better because she didn't want to
There is no justification
I completely agree with you.

## 146

She is the kind of mother to reveal it
Whatever you are trying to keep secret
If it's humiliating, she'll divulge it
She'll smile while you begrudge it
If it is the sons she won't say shit
But the daughter will have to hear it
What you deem personal she will surely leak it
Then pretend like she had nothing to do with it
She is in cahoots with your inner critic
But despite all the bullshit
You owned up to it
You know that she and her Terracotta Warriors are toxic
So why can't you force that evil woman into emotional
retirement?
Stop being hesitant
Constantly bending to her will certainly proves problematic
Aren't you tired of her behaving like she's some spectacular
religious psychic?
She will continue to spew the mean and inaccurate
But don't you dare buy it
Internalize it
Or
Resell it.

147

She's like an emotional black hole
Get too close and your soul will soon be stole
She devours your very being whole
Making your life as miserable as her life is
That's her primary is goal
What isn't apparent to them

To you is clearly known
Be cognizant of her
She is a black hole
Go.

### 148

No matter what you say
It didn't happen that way
You can never get to the truth
With all her lies in the way
She thinks her delusional denial is okay
And we know that karma is coming one day
But she lies so much
Why won't it arrive today?
I know a place where it can surely stay
And make that lying witch pay
For what she did yesterday
And is still doing day.

### 149

I'm certain she's crazy
Why can't anyone else see?
And none of her stories are rooted in reality
How could it possibly be?
But no one has the ovarian courage to admit it out loud but me
With her grimace smile she watches me bleed
But she carries a Bible
Guess who they'll believe?

### 150

With her stupid-ass rules I will no longer abide
It is too difficult to play that role when no one ever takes my
side

Never trust a mother that tries to make her own daughter
weak
The unthinkable I remembered
But she never encouraged or empowered me to speak
She never supported or approved
Even though acceptance I would seek
Sometimes I reflect on all of the time wasted and energy
A mother who never really wanted to know me
Controlling, controlling, controlling
While the animosity kept growing, growing and growing
She mistakenly wanted a clone
A duplicate is something that she wanted all along
With a mother like that
A daughter never belongs
And when it comes to believing her I'm always hesitant
And the fact that she birthed me is seriously irrelevant
She isn't who she pretends to be
Her low self-esteem and minute self-worth
She tried to push thank ridiculousness on to me
But I rejected it
Although whole she swallowed it
Comfortably indulging in the life of the tragic
And what she allowed and permitted
I wasn't having it
For my life today I am truly grateful and glad
I say it's been harder having an evil and demeaning mother
Than it is to have a pathetic dad
But her daughter is a poet
And she didn't even know
It was hidden
And now the daughters know it.


## 151


Constantly being coerced to feed that phony ego
Finally realizing that it is time to let her and her insanity go
She doesn't know that she is actually quite see through
All you want to do is just be peacefully you
Anything that doesn't serve her is always deemed to be
devilish and untrue

All the madness that she puts you through
Trying to convince herself that God loves her much more than
you
And she is ALWAYS trying to insinuate that she knows more
than you
Even when the evil witch doesn't have a clue
Recall all the years of negativity that she implanted into you
In fact,
Being a good mother is something that you haven't actually
ever seen her do
She may be helpful and supportive of them
But never of you
Her name is on your birth certificate
But that ain't hardly enough proof.

### 152

Those religious mothers tell you not to claim it
But don't you ever buy it
You are in a hospital bed
But she advises you not to say it
But ignore her crazy-ass
It is okay too claim it
And feel free to even rename it
If you don't acknowledge it
You will never be able to rise above it
Do not allow her insanity to leave you defeated
She has already ruined her own life
You can't fix it
She will have you believing that your diagnosis is illegitimate
That somehow your honesty makes you negligent
She will even try to convince you that your strength is an inner
impediment
That you should believe her lies just because she said it
And she'll even say that if you prayed more you wouldn't have
it

And if you aren't healed
It because of you!
Which will lead to your detriment
She thinks that God actually told her that
Take a moment to process that
She is a perpetually wrong religious zealot
If she can't have it
She will condemn it
Everyone is going to hell but her
If you let her tell it
And is envious because you persevered through every disappointment
You always manage to get up
And for over 60 years she has remained intellectually, emotionally, and financially stuck
Miserable, but enjoys criticizing you for getting out of your family rut
She's two-faced, but you have real guts
She loves using her faulty logic
And she tries to oppress you
But you keep getting up
She's mentally deficient,
But when it comes to common sense
You have more than enough
She represents what happens when religion runs amok
When it is time to be noble and honest she will surely induce her memory hiccups
She's jealous because you defeated EVERYTHING she couldn't buck
I've learned that blessings are truly real
But so is luck
So I push forward like Noah "40" Shebib who knows what it is like to have to be tough

And push forward even when those MS seas are physically rough.


## 153


If I could sit down and have dinner with anyone I'd choose me
Little girl who was always scared to death
I'm pick myself
My child-self
No one else
I'd want to tell her that it will all be okay
And that she'll have to recognize that her mother is the real obstacle in the way
And she has the right to have a say
It's her life anyway
I want her to know that she needs to go her own way
She needs to go far, far away
And realize that no truthfulness will her mother relay
Her mother will use dogma to try to make her stay
Bit I want my younger self to know that she's not obligated to play
That fake role about the perfect family
I want her to expect her mother to enforce a series of dream delays
And she will wrongly believe that everything has to be done exactly her way
And that her mother doesn't own her tomorrow or today
I'd tell her to learn to love and embrace every physical imperfection she wished away
And it is okay to go your own path even though her mother thinks it's not okay
I'd tell her that she was blessed with such a unique nose to smell and quickly identify the constant bullshit on display
And I'd tell her that relatives aren't necessarily family
And they are often the real enemies
And daughters can be the source of their mother's envy

And I'd use her extraordinary nose to sniff out the liars who
need not stay
I'd ask her to detect and avoid the maternal insanity on its way
She's ashamed to recognize what I rock everyday
And she isn't any more righteous than my younger self when
you pray
And one day it will be necessary to leave behind the mask
from the masquerade
And learn to appreciate the hairs that will one day turn gray
And all that matters is the fact that she is happy.

### 154

When you were younger she'd constantly pop the pimples on
my face
It started on 78th and Western Avenue when I was 8
And then she'd ask how your skin got that way
The evidence and damage you are still working to erase
Even in high school I couldn't make the scars go away
My friend said that it was because she wanted to purposely
and cruelly keep the boys away
Like when she whipped me with that extension cord in Carson
and made me wear shorts to an event the next say
I wonder to this very day.

### 155

She asks if I'm sure
She wants to ignore medicine and solely seek God for the
cure
Either or makes it all difficult to endure
Both combined will seemingly ensure
There are too many dead prayers for her ideology to seem
pure
Her two cents and crazy religious talk causes me to be
insecure
Her dogmatic stance is less inspiring and smells more like
manure

Removing her from the situation would be an improvement I'm sure
The exclusion of her two-cent is the secret cure
You alone own your body
She can't grant any unauthorized visits or preapproved tours.

## 156

They were called rolling blackouts
In an affluent and gated community
But we're the only dwelling with our lights out
Pretending like we can afford it
But I learned that all of the deception and dishonesty wasn't worth it
Even when the loans were intentionally defaulted
And the cars were being repossessed
We never discussed the fact that the daughter appeared distressed
Because there were people at the church she needed to impress
Forced to make imperfect lives appear spotless
It's exhausting professing to have more when you actually have less
A reality my mother still refuses to acknowledge and sanely profess.
What a mess.

## 157

I once asked it
Please stop visiting my ex I asked my mother
She was meeting with him constantly behind my back

And when I asked her to stop she said my request she'd only
"consider"
Daughters with good mothers never have to beg for loyalty
What is demanded of her isn't requirement for the other
Why isn't it that way for her brothers?
No valid excuse causes her to stutter
So she uses the mandates in the Bible to serve as her buffer
Why must a girl suffer?
It sucks being a daughter
When you have an evil and sexist mother.

## 158

I wasn't raised to keep up with the Jonses
I was raised to live for them.

He looks likes my father they say
And I resemble her anyway
So she worked to block every blessing in our way.

If it's a horrendous and poor financial decision
Best believe she'll surely grant her permission.

She will gladly help you ruin your credit
Teach you to spend what you don't have yet.

And when you make decisions that are smart
She claims that she and God don't want no part.

If you asked her to love her daughter
She wouldn't even know how to start.

Yet I am smart enough to live within my means

That antique gold digger doesn't know what that hell financial responsibility even means.

Spending like she got it
Hardly prepared for her retirement.

I was the adult even as a child
With a credit card I'm responsible and that witch still goes wild.

Old enough to know better
But she hasn't gotten any wiser.

No growth whatsoever
Same ole lies pretending like she's so cleaver
But I believe her never.

He'd leave time and time again after random interactions
But to this day she acts like none of that ever even happened
She pretends like it was my imagination
Or some kind of odd mental sensation.

I couldn't allow the constant lying and cruelty to persist
And as far as I'm concerned
That woman doesn't exist
She's been permanently dismissed
And will never be missed.

### 159

She lies
While looking you straight in your eyes
Between her and Pinocchio she demolishes any perceived tie
She's been a liar all your life

Never actually living what she preaches is right
So she finds new ways to stick her horrid behavior on Christ
Honesty and transparency she will never-ever attempt or try
Her strategy is just to remain dishonest and always deny
She'll try to make you believe that you aren't really seeing
what is before your eyes
She's the one holding you down while you're trying to rise
Always having a new financial emergency or surprise
She and a dollar can't live peacefully you realize
Worrying about what her daughter is spending on him
because she's worried about accessing her own supply
So if her daughter gives her less money she'll pretend to know
why
Talking behind his back was something she never should
have tried
She's never pays, but must be the only passenger on any ride
Always talking about forgiveness when I know those she's
pushed aside
She's always ridden the waves of the animosity tide
That witch is lying and she knows she isn't right
Under her no decent daughter can happily survive
You've spent way too much critical time
Giving her bullshit and backwards-ass thinking the opportunity
to shine
She believes that women should crawl and beg and never
climb
She's a woman with a sick and oppressive mind
She the type of scoundrel that recreates the same ridiculous
situations and lame alibis
She thinks she can camouflage the stench of bullshit with
oregano and thyme
But you and I have evaluating and interpreting all the clear
signs

A real woman would never cross those lines
She really needs to resign
And hand over the labia because she's committed way too
many maternal crimes
She repeats the same bad behavior that she always manages
to somehow to justify
Everything is always deniable and worth a deceptive lie
She undermines a great education when she works overtime
to keep her own daughter emotionally and psychologically
stuck
She could never be a halfway decent mother to her daughter
because she didn't have the guts
Her early 1900's view of the world drove you completely nuts
I see why you don't give a flying fuck!
She's just too much
You are the daughter of a mother who has long proven to be
your smiling rival
You're always at your apex
And she's always working to topple
She's always trying to insight a new jealousy laced verbal
squabble
And is never held by others to be justifiably responsible
So anything that she may say at this point is purely laughable
You've deemed that witch to be certifiably intolerable
And any reconciliation attempts are absolutely and
unquestionably nonnegotiable
You live to be happy
She exists purely to be hurtful
Girl, I don't blame you.

160

I love my life!

Even though I have a psycho mother who has never been fair or mentally right.

When you are born in that kind of skin
And you make it known that she is someone that you really can't stand
Some may wrongly perceive your Mommy Dearest admission to be the ultimate sin.

Well, I play to win
So no matter what they may think or the stories they may spin
A truthful conversation about crazy-ass mothers and wronged daughters is one I am willing to begin.

I remember once when my father told me to do the dishes since the guys wanted to watch the game
My mother agreed with him and advised me to do the same
With my brothers looking on
You can only imagine my understandable anger and inner shame.

The fact that he'd said something so misogynist and cruel really, really pissed me off
But the fact that my mother encouraged it
Well, that proved to be so much more tough.

I knew then that I was in this "family"
But I knew that I would be the lone casualty
That not even my mother would help me.

So as soon as I could I left her house forever
There was nothing safe that I could ever divulge or tell her

She worked to make everything in my life worse when she
could have made it better.


Determined that my mother's miserable and phony life I'd
never be prone
And despite all of the toxicity she ensured that I was shown
I set out on my path alone
And despite her constant hating and the non-support of my
"family"
I've matured and grown
And there is peace, love and gender equality here
Unlike in her dysfunctional and oppressive home.



My father even once mentioned when I was a teenager
That my mother didn't like me
Back then I wondered how that could be
Was her behavior really as transparent to others as it clearly
seemed?
That witch is the original Ice Queen
As cold and unemotional as ice cream
Sometimes her anger and hostility was hard for me to believe
To this day her fake saintly behavior baffles and confuses me
Holding a Bible, but dumbly carrying out every evil deed
By observing her I've learned never to trust only what you can
see
And don't always believe that people are who they pretend to
be
He may have lived dual lives,
But her boarders were also super cloudy
I existed under twisted and make believe religious canopy
I worked tirelessly to keep that crazy and evil bitch happy
Even though she always perceived me as her primary enemy

I tried to look past her insanity
I tried to ignore her sheer lack of maternal credibility
She tried to squash the self-esteem in me she'd learn to envy
I guess because when it came to self-love and self-respect
She didn't have any
She tried
But I wouldn't allow her to destroy me
She always had a difficult time encouraging and supporting
me
And it annoys her to know that what she tried to destroy kept
on surviving
And kept on thriving
And advancing
I always knew what she was late at realizing
My success was destined despite all of her discouragements
and sabotaging
My attitude towards her should not be surprising
And I did it ALL without compromising
I strongly dislike that witch every fiber of my being
No one who REALLY knows me will find my emotions
shouldn't be surprising.
And, oh yeah, the fight you and Larry had in Carson happened
Stop denying and lying!

161

You have gained and accomplished more than she ever did
But she's still complaining
Isn't that weird?
She is always criticizing and hating!
Even when you expect her to be kind and accepting
Every time you think that she'll be satisfied
You are always mistaking and left mystified

Negativity and financial chaos is something she just loves creating
And if you are waiting for her to be eventually pleased
You will be forever waiting
Any energy you give to that emotional pariah
That evil witch is taking!
So when it comes to your happiness stop ignoring
You deserve to be happy
Please stop foregoing.

## 162

My arc set sail long ago
Where it leads?
I'm excited to know
I am strong enough to go there alone
She must be kept on a leash and never be permitted to roam
Thank God I'm finally wiser and officially grown!
I'll be a braver and more courageous woman than the one I was always shown
Society's single impression isn't the only mother-daughter relationship known
Our truth also deserves to be poetically interpreted and not thrown
Our experiences are valid and nothing we say or feel is overblown
We are the daughters of living mothers who chastise the perfume
But embolden and champion for only the cologne
A girl like me couldn't excel in that kind of zone
It was hell in her home
Daughters,

I know I'm not alone.

## 163

She is forgiven without repentance
You ask them
I'm the menace
But I'm the one met within indifference
She imposes antiquated rules disguised as religion
For far too long I've been imprisoned
Allowing her to weigh in on my decisions
While listening to her sexist and cruel reasons
She can't stay
Even some mothers are only for a season.

## 164

I can be the nicest person you ever could know
Until you bring up that woman
Then a different side I quickly show
It's difficult being the only one in a family willing to be honest
The one with the proof who can identify the lies and every
broken promise
It's tiring
A daughter should admire her mother
But for me there is no admiring
What I wanted her to become I'm officially retiring
I've tried to get it
I even tried buying
I'm done trying
She ain't welcome here
My poems have made that crystal clear
And I advise them all to stand clear
Especially when the only non-liar is near
Their two cents and excuses?

I can't even hear.

## 165

We are survivors!
And we made it without her
We advocated for our own rights
We didn't wait for that fairy tale or magical knight
In her ruthless home
There was no separation between church and State
Since religion determined our very state
It even affected our very own fate
So on our very own bodies we would sometimes retaliate
You can't trust your own mother enough to tell her about that
sexual abuse or that rape
The only thing she knows about you is your name
Beyond that she'll draw a complete blank
We feel like being born to her was a huge mistake
We often imagine what could have been and how things could
have been great
For the day we can leave we anxiously wait, and wait, and
wait
Besides that physical feature we share no other traits
No matter my view she can't relate
Our basic rights we have to keep secret or cleverly negotiate
Birth control access or condoms isn't something we could ever
communicate
Everything that matters at that age she's the keeper of every
gate
And her ridiculous daughter rules she constantly dictates
She thinks that she's so much more divine than us and we're
the evil apostate
Over our own lives we don't even have the right to evaluate

Or methods are contorted and only her methodology is
straight
For too long we've eaten off her poisonous plate
We joined the other escaped daughters before it was too late
Now we are awake
And when we spoke our truth it was like a quake!
For her submissive and degrading way of living we could no
longer be a candidate
I see us all the same
We are merely pawns in her game
She uses us for her own amusement and sadistic gain
We struggle to be us while dismissing the insanity and sexist
ways we were "trained"
If it's physical there is a number you can anonymously and
while unidentifiably draped in shame
But when the abuse from your mother is emotional and
psychological
Daughters like us aren't given a name
Present mothers can be far more damaging than absent
fathers
If for your wedding she can't bother
You have your answer girl
Look no further.

## 166

Just because I'm nice
Doesn't mean you get to stay in my midst eternally or for life
I haven't seen him in 20 years
But you continue to enforce the patriarchal system he
perpetuated through fear
Every time you visit I shed a tear
Because I absolutely HATE, HATE, HATE having you here!
I can be myself and I can't think clear

You are the monster that your father was to you and that's so unfortunate and weird
The only difference between you two is the beard
I've stated my case a zillion times and I'm tired of talking about it.
My faux-family can go ahead and debate or stupidly doubt it
But there will be NO more conversations
These poems clearly state my position
Complete detachment is my intention
Continue reading if you are still confused about my necessary reaction
On my part there will be no more inaction
I want you closely understand my denunciations
I will no longer be a daughter-slave on your planation
And in cutting you completely off
There is no hesitation
Understand that this isn't one of your typical crazy hallucinations
Through your eyes and to your brain I want there to be absolute penetration
YOU DO NOT OWN ME!
THANKFULLY,
I AM NOT YOU!
I'm tired of being ridiculed and I'm exhausted from the continuous humiliations
From you and your evilness
I'm taking a long awaited and much deserved permanent vacation.

167

I am no longer afraid
To tell my daughter story
I'm worthy
I can already hear the excuses and lies you'll prepare
Forever emotionally unavailable
The relationship that I rightfully deserve is clearly unattainable
I will no longer be available

Despite you
I know that I'm loveable
You are the one that's disgraceful
And finally telling you what I think of you
Well, that's absolutely delectable!

## 168

Since I was little I knew
I knew what I wouldn't do
I knew that I'd never end up mean and bitter like you
Why'd you have a daughter if you couldn't see the
requirements through?
Raising her with an unfair sense of obligation
Those idiotic and sexist rules had nothing to do with her
But they had everything to do with you.

## 169

I take responsibility for who I am and what I've done
But I am the ONLY one
You tell the truth and they come undone
They try to discredit you because you aren't a son
Her Terracotta Warriors protecting the most unholy and phony
one
When you are the one that's positive
It is difficult being around all that negative
You have the right to tell your story
They protect the structure of the patriarchal family
The healing of the daughters is the objective
Our truth isn't relative
Silence is equivalent to ingesting a sedative

Acknowledge the injury
I refuse to listen to anymore lies designed to attack my
credibility
You know what you did to me
You know that without you it couldn't be
You sucked out my energy
And shitted on me like I was your personal laboratory
But I'm still telling MY story
You can't keep me from my glory
All the suffering daughters now know me
For once, we aren't the ones who should worry
That apology and recognition you owed
You should have hurried.

## 170

Don't take any credit for the daughter you raised
You had absolutely nothing to do with the outstanding woman
she became
She did it all without naming any names
But those who truly know her have learned that you are to
blame
A new successor has been strategically named
We are all happy to witness the end of your daughter-hating
reign
Freedom prevents the continuation of life in your designer
chains
You are not innocent or as goodhearted as you claim.

## 171

We can't blame it mostly on our fathers
What he dealt in our minds in the farthest

No props for the daughter who has consistently worked the hardest
The sons are noteworthy,
But even the recognition of the girl's medical accomplishments is noticeably modest
She loves picking on the only girl each daily harvest
She tries destroying her inner will and dedication because her spirit is the largest
To the daughter Lucifer and her mother are synonymous
She was born unto a mother who is visibly heartless
An ice queen that has proven to be extremely callous
That daughter will eventually win regardless
She can't be stopped
Just like us.

172

I am unrepentant
I am enthusiastically admitting it
I am gallantly addressing it
I'm not afraid of you or it
I'm writing it
I'm saying it
You'll deny it
There's no doubting it
But it would be in your best interest not to try it
All that matters is that I like it.

173

Always trying to one up you
She's can't brag about herself
So she compares you two
Always worried about the pockets of others

And what someone else can do
Always working her saintly voodoo
Always stirring her homemade concoctions into her witch's
brew
All these years my anger against you has stewed
You do everything a pious woman and faux-Christian should
not do
A mother who oppresses her daughter
What does that say about you?
But this observation is nothing new
You'll pretend to be the martyr as always
And you'll wrongly that I'm being called tactless and crude
When you're actually the one being rude
But I have a right to have an attitude
I had a mother like you!
You try being the daughter of a woman who REFUSES to see
or hear you
There was nothing else to do
You proved that no one is immune from being deceived and
lied to
The moment you opened your mouth
I knew that shit wasn't true.


<u>174</u>


You will not be her jinx
Watch what she will ultimately be
She recognizes what you are unable to see
Her belief in herself spans into infinity
You purposely caused her so much distress and misery
She provided proof and you still didn't believe
Why couldn't you just let her be?
She had to leave

What happened to her also happened to me.

## 175

In her abnormal cathedral,
She won't acknowledge you.

Though I caught a glimpse of her on the dank mattress,
Realizing then that she's a rather unconvincing actress.

She is both evil and needy,
Life for her is all about me, me, me.

Age doesn't necessarily mean that she knows more than you,
Their phoniness conceals the fact that you are surrounded by
a plethora of old fools.

It is impossible to have a relationship with her Terra-Cotta
Warriors and defenders,
To advocate for her madness you have to be an accomplished
pretender.

Being the daughter of an unhappy and unstable mother is
filled with constant drama,
But don't expect her to take any responsibility for her role in
the trauma.

Don't let them make you feel guilty!
It's all about you now
Your distance from her and her Terra-Cotta Warriors is the
necessary penalty.

Be constantly aware of her recognizable maternal
shortcomings,

They'll try the same ole' guilt trip,
But don't you go back running.

### 176

An apology from him equates to mere purses and shoes
For her
That kind of semi-apology will do
But for her daughter
Materialism isn't what's due
The ridiculous accumulation of stuff leaves her oddly happy
and abnormally amused
But the purchase of things isn't how you heal a heart and
relationship that has been bruised
But that's what she's into
But I won't be made to feel used
For her a designer purse is worth the black and blue
Choosing materialism over respect is what she taught me to
do
As if stuff and things is some way for him to prove
That the mistreatment only masks the fact that he loves you
Like money somehow results in the wrong behavior being
removed
I'm glad that I dropped out of her oppressive daughters school
For her
Monetary gain and the purchase of non-necessities will always
do
That's the way a man gets through
But being bought off I refused to do
I'm mastering being a woman and she still doesn't have any
clue
Her sick and twisted way of living was not for neither me or
you

She acts like what those other women tolerate she could
never do
But I've always wanted to ask
How are they any different from you?
Especially since you both end up getting screwed.

## 177

She enjoys living her prized false life
Off her daughter's strength and confidence she will surely
capitalize
She is envious of her daughter's ability to live without
compromise
And her daughter's inner fight and will to joyfully survive
By the dollar signs her daughter has never been hypnotized
But money is all you see while looking into her mother's eyes
To get what she wrongly thinks she deserves she'll steadily
terrorize
Her mother's cruelty is predictable and her unrelenting anger
comes at no surprise
And for her and her faux-family the daughter no longer has the
appetite
She now knows that she will never attempt to make that
mother-daughter relationship right
A daughter is useless when a mother is only seduced by
homes, cars, and bright lights
Any physically uncivil and emotionally abusive man with
money is her mother's type
She taught her daughter to lay down with that kind of man at
night
And always do what he says since men have that ridiculous
right
Mothers like that are of a rather peculiar type
And as long as he pays the bills no daughter should have a
gripe
Just when we are happy and at peace in the light
Here she comes prepared to strike
Ready to show us what jealousy and bitterness looks like.

A town where everybody knows everyone
Can be a place where everyone knows no one
Just because she birthed me
Doesn't mean that she knows me
I'm foreign
The phony smile I no longer adorn
I've stopped saying I love you
I will no longer feel pressure to say what I know not to be true
Those days are over
I grow prouder of myself every day that I grow older.

179

I don't see her as a mother
I see her a dark phase
Crawling my way out of her oppressive dysfunction proved to
be an intricate and quite confusing maze
Oh, the road to womanhood I found to be astonishingly jagged
and purposely unpaved
Her twisted church doctrine keeps girls ridiculously focused on
the grave
Always focused on the heaven of tomorrow and never the hell
she's creating today
I'm gleefully on the outside now and I refuse to participate in
the games that she and my faux-family like to play
Acting like no offense has a name
I never buy what I can't afford and she rarely purchases what
she can realistically afford to pay
It's always about her and never about what I think and say
I learned from myself that ovaries are beneficial and testicles
can often get in the way
Ovaries help me to detect the cryptic insults and the subtle
faultfinding hidden within the things she likes to say

Her lack of integrity means that wherever the money lives she
will surely sway
For a woman it is never decent to say
But for a man everything is okay
To her a "good daughter" is only one who obeys
She can't relate to any courageous and secure woman doing it
her way
But the daughters out there know that her subservience will
lose to my happiness every single day
Although I wish there could have been another way
But life determined it necessary to be this way
In my life she could never be permitted to stay
I refuse to allow her gloomy clouds to reign over my day
No more
No way.

## 200

No one knows that I'm a poet
But me
I'm the only one who knows it
Hands over mouths with eyes bulging
I can seem them reading it
Shocked that I actually had the ovaries to say it
She thought she hid it
And they thought the covered it
But the daughters know that we don't have to forget it
They can't tell us how to deal with it
They will be amazed that I had the guts to broadcast it
Astounded that I'd actually admit to it
That to everyone I am confessing it
They'll be shocked to learn that my mother is emotionally
illiterate
In a book no less!
In my mind their reaction I can already see
But I'm proud of myself for revealing my truth about what is
purely connected to me
NO ONE owns me or my peculiar story
It is impossible for her to instill any more fear into me

I'm just painting my specific picture in words
Now, it's all about the daughters and me
The mother-daughter relationships that never could be
Although I tried solely
I tried working on it independently
Even my faux-family has tried to persuade me
When no one listened to us
We still survived it - - luckily
It's the experience of the misled daughters I am telling
Through poetry, our cohesive realities I am weaving
It ended this way because of the beginning
Truthfulness to those type of people is equivalent to sinning
The losers in the circle are made to appear winning
But we are unyielding
There is no ceiling
But through silence, it is our honesty and right to speak that
they are stealing
She forced her way onto these pages even when I wasn't
willing
And once I started writing
My soul I began spilling
I spend countless hours reconsidering
The approval and concurrence I once wanted from her
I'm no longer needing
For me integrity and honesty were far too appealing
After all of the constant bombardment of her criticisms and
judgments there could be no more delaying
Her closed book of spells and twisted scriptures I'm finally
opening
And then it became emotionally necessary to write about her
lies and double-dealing
And through poetry I will tell the story of the mistreated
daughters and our upbringings
And I want to tell the daughters like me to stop expecting any
sincere apologies
We will challenge the world to understand what our family
systems are communities intentionally ignoring
The fact that you can still have a sexist household with no
father in it is repulsive and appalling
Since I've experienced it

I'm knowing
Bad mothers keep the misogyny going
Inflicting sadistic emotional pain through their ongoing bullying
We're going to speak it anyway
Through my poetic stanzas I'm determined to sincerely and
honestly tell our stories
Poetically and courageously
Many daughters feel this way
I've learned that it is not just me.


## 201


The sons
She empowers to do more
Then sabotages the daughter's attempts to get too far
I know who you are
Daughters like us still wishing on a star
Every best attempt is considered by her to subpar
Always looking over your shoulder and keeping your slightly
door ajar
She's always there
Criticizing and comparing you to everything from afar
Your weight, your hair, your body, your car
She's the first one with the feathers and the bucket of tar
I know who you are
We have the same meticulous emotional scares.


## 202


I'm so over it!
Now I just ignore it
The great distance is for my own happiness and betterment
That plane ticket?
I suggest that you not get
The front door?
I won't be opening it

I really need you to finally get it
Your feelings are irrelevant
And my past desires to please you was just symptomatic
Of a bigger issue much more dramatic
The answer is always no because the question is always
encased in bullshit
Enabling and perpetuating those family lies
I'm just not with it.

## 203

I hate engaging with and absorbing the news
There is always a vast selection and abundance of
unfortunate circumstances and morbid views
The "pick your sadness" game I'm expertly used to
With a mother like ours
I know you can relate too
Always knowing exactly what to say and what to do
Always working to keep the heat off of you
You survive dinners with her by paying your way through
That means paying her tab too
Your siblings feel like that's the least you can do
They serve as her Terra-Cotta Warriors and don't even really
know you
But inside you are screaming
FUCK YOU!
Reading from a script you didn't write or approve
Just pretending to be engaged like your mother would do
Carefully choosing the least painful option for you
But only no news is good news
Silence and obliviousness is okay to sometimes choose
It's them
And there is absolutely nothing wrong with you
You have absolutely nothing to prove

It's great living a life without the world's constant and
depressing doomsday news
They wish they had the ability to ignore and deflect like you
Me too.

204

She's glad she didn't listen
She's so glad that she didn't let you instigate complications
Before she'd reluctantly halt any inner hesitations
Afraid to declare her own proclamation
Discouraged from seeking her own emancipation
But this is real life and void of her meaningless mother-like
impressions
Motherhood is a role for life
She clearly lacks the dedication.

205

So she met him online
So what?
Get with the times!
The number of girlfriends your husband had could form a
lengthy line
She could drop a whole lot of dimes!
Always criticizing some else's happy and secure life
Look at yours!
It surely doesn't entice
A mother with a heart for her daughter comparable to the size
of a grain of rice
A nasty demeanor
But with you out of the picture
She's able to keeps hers relaxed and so very nice

The shit you do should keep you up at night
You're mean to your own daughter
But around them you act all phony and ultra-polite
But you swear you are the one living in the light
Everyone else is wrong and you are the only one right
Steadily trying to dim her light
Don't you get tired of always being wrong when she's always right?
You aren't all that bright
So you inject the Bible into every discussion to purposely force a disagreement or fight
Jealous of your own daughter
That's not right
And if you didn't hear her now
She'll happily say it twice.

## 206

They don't know what it's like
Living under that kind of spite
Never having any rights
A place where being a girl is considered impolite
Praying for the painful and heavy menstruation to cease every night
Keeping secrets because she and her mother aren't tight
A mother who claims that motherhood is a woman's main purpose and it should remain in sight
But not every girl wants that life
She's never had that maternal feeling that can claim a woman's life
Never wanted to be a mother, but definitely a wife
She's a spectacular type
The forgotten daughters she will ignite

She's always felt her purpose inside
The decision to be childless is her right
Whichever way a woman goes is alright
A mother should never steer a daughter left when she knows
she should go right
Every woman should have the human right to choose her own
life
Mothers still playing God in their adult daughters' lives
That just ain't right.

## 207

Your favorite artist will put the individual in a song
In my writings they belong
What is written on paper becomes etched in stone
Words on paper is where my communications belong
Here I can write every single wrong
She kept pushing me
So I knew then that it wouldn't be long
Even if some disagree
I'm saying what I felt all along
For those sins against me she must atone
I just want to be left alone.

## 208

Destined for a life of misery and servitude
To him and kids and never to you
That's what that kind of mother will do
She'll teach her daughter that she has to
That's just what women are "supposed" to should do
They mistakenly prepare daughters for life designed to be
unfair and spiritually untrue
But to that sexist and demeaning ideology she is attached by
glue

And her only sense of purpose in life is derived from a series
of oppressive gender rules
A different way I always knew I would choose
I closely observed her unpleasant, abusive, and regimented
life as a woman and I wasn't enticed or amused
I knew that a repeat of her life I could never-ever approve
I guess since she was so unhappy and miserable she wanted
to punish me too
Saying she was pleased by her choices didn't mask our
mother-daughter truth
That's fine if you want that for you
But what about the daughters who are forced when they
clearly don't want to?


## 209


Constant fear
When she speaks you've learned to cover your ears
For as long as you can remember she's told you that the end
is near
But the self-assured and unafraid daughters have survived
decades of suffering through her campaign of daily fear
And despite her curses of doom we're still here
She can't understand why God keeps blessing us and giving
us the all clear
Her new cycle of last days begins anew with every New Year
And every new January 1st she's perplexed when she sees
that we're still alive and happy and continuously reappear
Especially since she predicted our demise last year
She claims that every new human catastrophe is a reflection
of God's unhappiness or long-awaited cheer
She claims to be God's spokesperson even though love,
acceptance, and peace isn't something that we never-ever
hear

So she uses dread and fear of the unknown to swiftly kick our
positivity and inspirational stance in the rear
Acceptance and pure love aren't activities or beliefs to which
she could ever adhere
So, if there's one thing I could tell you, Daughter Dear
It's never, never, never let your mother grab your life's steering
wheel and steer
If you do
Tomorrow you won't be here.

## 210

I stop letting her fuck up my chill
Before she opens her mouth
I already know the deal
She doesn't give two fucks about how I feel
Countless times I've experienced and marched to her
psychotic drills
Being her daughter has always been a battle fought uphill
Hours before her visit I'm grabbing the anti-anxiety pills
I am her preferred thing to grill
And to her false relics and twisted maternal logic she expects
me to kneel
For 40 years I felt too powerless to exert my own will
Even after telling her what transpired
She maintains an expression of cruel and heartless steel
Yet I can immediately feel her presence making me ill
How'd I end up with a mother who loves going in for the kill?
Danger headed towards her daughter and she sits strangely
still
How can she remain as stoic as a face on a currency bill?
For mercy and support I used to appeal
Now I see her as an unnecessary third wheel

In my eyes
Her fate has been unceremoniously sealed
I refuse to listen any longer to her conniptions and erratic
religious shrills
She wants my life to be her sequel
Our tastes are too dissimilar to share any womanly meal
The life I worked for she has always tried to steal
I've already made known the deal
I will never again allow her ruin my necessary chill.


## 211


She and the news will ruin your faith in humanity
So both I try to always ignore and disagree
Constantly peddling the same old ideologies
The intersection between race and gender can make for
interesting chemistry
A balance of unique synergies
Two different loyalties
I create my own theories
Sometimes what they may think really doesn't mean shit to me
As a woman I can't wholeheartedly agree
I too know women of that same shade who can't breathe
Their lives matter too
But they're dead or living life on their knees
For as far as the human eye can see
It's happening globally
Woman and girls all over the world are being destroyed by our
own systematic disease
Mothers utilizing gender roles define what a girl deserves and
needs
Trading her for money and status makes our hearts bleed

In the grand scope what she wants is as miniscule as a
pepper seed
Finding a husband and birthing kids is all they are ever taught
us to see
Our own mothers steering us to dangerous men whose hearts
are encased in weeds
Forget education or the chance to attain that highest degree
With that experience and that paper comes independence and
power they refuse to see
They think that everything they're fed is really reality
They believe what is on their TV and on their computer
screens
Sometimes it just makes me want to scream
Daughters mindlessly watching
But I know what this all means
They start believing in the "life" that they see
Daughter begin to believe that it is all as wonderful as it seems
Like there is shame in using your brain to propel your dreams
Don't allow your money-hungry mother to trade you to another
team
Don't allow the accumulation of material things be your
everything
Make your intelligence and wisdom supreme
Money alone should never make your heart gleam
Demand more from life and redirect any negative energy
Yeah, your mother will surely exhibit animosity
But still do it with sincerity
Because if you don't
You are living illogically
And doing it her way will induce a cosmic penalty
I know
Because it happened to me.

What she tells them is never true
But you can't control what she may or may not say about you
You already know that lying and embellishing is what she'll do
It is something you just get uncomfortably used to
It annoys the hell out of us daughters too
But don't let her negativity affect what you must accomplish
and do
See your goal through
At a certain point it stops being about her
And it becomes about you
So, what will you do?

213

We have emotionally battered daughter's syndrome
Sometimes she's nice to us
So they encourage us to leave it alone
It's always been that way in her home
Every time you walk through those doors all of your arcane
emotional scars are shown
You seem perfect
Who would have even known?
Too scared to leave because her verbal abuse is all you've
ever known
So you endure the verbal insults and criticisms because to her
she thinks you belong
Afraid to protect yourself and leave
Afraid of being alone
So you just go along.

214

That pea-brained crap never made any sense to me
No one will tell me what I have to do or what to be
I live quite simply
She does her and I gladly do me
I've tried to put it delicately
I've tried countless times to be kind and even friendly
But she wouldn't leave me be
She made me
I couldn't take any more insults and prodding
By that book I'm not abiding
I won't endure anymore preaching and chiding
So now I'm writing
A mother who has already given up on life
Will never understand or appreciate a daughter who keeps on
trying.

## 215

I've always seen that type of relationship as a trap
When it's time to move forward
You have psychical evidence but her Terracotta Warriors try to
force you back
Wanting to depart, but to that obligation you are strapped
Too scared to say that you never wanted that
Unlike her
You weren't going to be anyone's doormat
Your father said to never bring a baby into his home
And he meant that
For over 20 years
You and birth control pills and uterine devises have had an
unspoken contract
Every day of your life you two made contact

And to your mother's gender enforcements you'd always counteract
She loved preaching about the dangers birth control pills and how estrogen ensures physical havoc
But with subservience you'd refuse to react
And even to this day
Your chosen motherless stance is something she still attacks
But your hysterectomy proved to be the permanency needed to officially deflect
Any attempts by her to make you feel negligent
The necessary surgery kept your promise to yourself in tact
You and your intuition made a definitive pact
And you refused to allow her to control any of that
Oh, how she wishes that you and your menstrual suffering could make contact
But your life has never worked like that
She's sees the purpose of a woman's life to be exclusively tied to some cryptic biblical pact
And the suffering and burden of a woman is an unfair myth derived from her religious sect
Dogma dictates what's proper and what's inept
She wrongly assumed that her daughter would change her mind or is putting on some sort of act
Children is NOT how that adult daughter chooses to interact
There is absolutely NOTHING wrong with that
Not all women want babies
I know that to be a certain fact
She made that declaration when she was very young
And she meant every word and she never looked back
She remained steadfast despite the attacks
She always knew that her life would never involve that
And she wasn't meant for that
She's right where she planned and predicted she'd to be at

How can you fault her for that?
When she said no
She clearly meant exactly that
Get back.

## 216

When she's tired
She's tired
I suggest no one bothers
She hates gossip and hearing plans to conspire
She'll employ you today
And tomorrow you're surprisingly fired
In solitude her mind climbs higher
Relaxed is her preferred attire
Herself
She's learned to love, respect, and admire
She has defeated the liar
Today she shines as bright as a sapphire
She too is a daughter.

## 217

Not everything was or is your father's fault
Not every problem hides in in his blame vault
That's the bullshit your mother taught
If you subscribe to that theory
Her carefully choreographed lies you've already bought
Begin to question what you have been told and taught
Use your brain
To unlock your inner vault.

## 218

I've said YES for far too long

I was made to feel that the word NO is somehow mean or
wrong
I heard that women and the word NO just don't get along
But the word NO is what makes daughters like us strong
The word NO will remove an insincere smile from a requesters
face
While protecting you from some of your mother's dysfunction
and disgrace
NO has proven over and over again to be my saving grace
It stops me from agreeing when I know I have no place
Time and energy are valuable and NO shields me from waste
YES will have you in crap up to your waist
Unable to figure out how it uncontrollably got this way
The word NO always secures for me what the word YES
seeks to erase
I've learned the hard way to make NO commonplace
I now say it without haste
It may be bitter initially
But through practice it will become an acquired taste
Make no mistake
When they hear NO instead of the YES they've grown to
anticipate
They'll do a double-take
The bravery to say NO
Girl, learn to cultivate and appreciate.


<u>219</u>


Born to never make waves
Another he or him to worship is always deemed okay
A system designed to dictate where a female must surrender
and lay

Those redundant anti-women ideologies that always get in our way
The rules our mothers forced us to follow everyday
We never consented to eating off that sexist and tainted tray
Everything we are force-fed is way beyond the expiration date
The inedible portions emotionally and psychologically starved daughters are forced to intake
Mothers ignore the spiritual malnourishment of their daughters since they wrongly equate sustenance with weight
Sometimes it's just too much to take
The example she has set we refuse to emulate
We are the brave daughters who refuse to just sit idly by and just wait
Allowing our mothers to determine for us the man allowed to impregnate
Especially when we know in our hearts that her interference is a mammoth mistake
Our mothers enjoy telling us that we can't have it that way
Since what was uncaringly written thousands of years ago about females is accurate today
Our required submission and obedience to the disrespectful and brutish we must always obey
Our mothers tell us that it must always be that way
But that makes absolutely no sense to us in any way
Mothers should want the best for their daughters
But they rush to be the first to say okay
It isn't our fault
But our boldness and courageousness is confirmation to her of our blame
Since that apple in the garden we've always been marked and named
Just being a female comes with a historical and traditional level of shame

Our own mothers are double agents who've thrown us into that skewed game
And decades later we decide that it isn't okay to emulate the same
I know sons never chastised when their deceptions cause family stains
But a daughters strength and determination instigates sunny skies to rain
So our bravery is all that remains
When we tell our mothers and families that the unfair interest rate for being a daughter is vacuous to pay
Yet daughters are encouraged by their own disconnected mothers to stay
In situations and with people who aren't okay
Nice and sweet is always the game we are encouraged to play
They're looking at him
But our mothers should be admonished for the things that they do and say
Like mistreated daughter own them a slice of cake!
When all they've ever done is take, take, take
Daughters with good mothers can't relate
But daughters like us exist and it may be hard for some to contemplate
Yet we ride the courageous waves we were told never to make
We've decided not to just blindly or idiotically obey
Just because it's always been that way
Well mothers, it's a new day
Daughters are determined to have it all their way
I've received and accomplished EVERYTHING that I ever wanted because of what I had the courage to admit and say
When my mother doubted and discouraged I still found a way
We are the daughters who live for ourselves today

As long as we approve
Our aspirations and desires won't be delayed
The expenses for our bravery has already been paid
In front of the universe our meticulous plans have been
detailed and laid
Construction has begun and our personal building plans were
approved today
And the final draft didn't require our mother's signature or okay
Our own mothers tried to stop us from making the necessary
waves
And when we didn't know any better we would just authorize
and okay
But now we immaculately surf life's chaotic waves
Successfully managing everything that comes our way
We appreciate our place in the world every single day
And what they refused to conquer
We've had the courage to both acknowledge and triumphantly
slay
We will *Kick Push* like Lupe
Don't tell us there isn't a way
Touché!


220


If I had a daughter
I'd want her to be like me
Sovereign, faithful, and loving
True to herself and what she's called to be
And always listen to her intuition emphatically
All the while knowing that she creates her latest destiny
And knowing when to walk away when it ain't got shit to do
with me
I'd want a daughter as loyal and kind as me

While knowing when to advocate for herself and other women
when others refuse to see
Always giving even when much is taken from me
Staying positive despite the life's latest catastrophe
Always choosing her circle, associates, and friends carefully
A daughter who knows herself intimately
It doesn't matter the circumstance, misfortune or the disease
She'd bring every opposition to her purpose to its knees
If I had a daughter like me I'd be relieved
A woman who won't live the life of the peeved
A courageous daughter who truly believes
And is cognizant of those who seek to deceive
A daughter whose uterus will never make her grieve
A daughter is aware and avoids the family's misdeeds
A daughter who moves full speed
Ahead of those who refuse to accept reality so they
perpetually grieve
A daughter who is weary of those who cry me, me, me
I forgave even my mother tried to sabotage me
And imposed her unjustifiable criticisms birthed through
religiosity
I stood up for myself when no one else would defend me
And my words and actions proved credibility
Despite a family that's always wishy-washy
I never asked for anything
But was always giving them everything
Yet she criticized me for doing what was necessary
I had to amputate the leeches to stop the bleeding
I'd want a daughter who is courageous despite the weakness
she would always see
I'd be happy and not jealous of her ability to climb even higher
than me

I'd be proud of my daughter for not becoming another family casualty
And for not allowing him to induct her into a life of misery
I'd be proud of her for choosing to be happy
And for not using religion to mask the torture and melancholy
And for becoming the type of woman who knows not to trust everybody
And for rebuffing the controlling
For doing what she believed
And for admonishing lying
For making wise decisions and living incredibly
And I'd congratulate her when her life displays her enlightened learning
I'd be proud of her and admire her discovery
I'd be proud of her for being a girl and for living unapologetically
And for being able to exist independently
And for knowing that internally she encompasses dependability
Never needing money or asking for material things from me
But I was never enough for my mother you see
Yet, I'm more than enough for me
I'm a great daughter undisputedly
I'm a much better daughter than the one she used to be
And despite my mother and father I'm living happy and successfully
I'm proud of myself
For not allowing her to define me
I'm proud of me
The me you now see
A daughter built perfectly
Because she's right internally.

Whenever what you have to say is already considered
irrelevant
To speak the truth we are always hesitant
For years we've been on trial and still no suitable or fair
settlement
Your life is ruled under her odd translation of the Old and New
Testament
Religious theories that infer that woman deserve to be
stagnant
But that's not even the worse of it
Still accepting her mean and judgmental temperament
But what we know is so prevalent
The mistreatment and brainwashing of daughters is rampant
Escape from her cult behavior was for our own betterment
Even your pedophile and abusive father couldn't take it
So imagine the overwhelming nature it
We've learned that keeping the peace can be a dangerous
sentiment
A story of a baby girl who's worth at birth is already spent
A vagina can automatically make a daughter an oppressed
bargaining chip
To live her life independently she is intentionally unequipped
Her mother saw to it
You can't run if you can't see it
For being born she thinks you automatically owe it
But we'd probably pay if what's required from a mother she'd
at least show a little of it
She's lying again and we already know it
After hearing the same dogmatic script for years one starts to
ignore it
Your butt is on you

Yet, she feels like she rightfully owns it
Over your life your discriminatory mother has always been president
You've existed for decades under her sole dictatorship
And the perception of others holds every seat in her narcissistic parliament
Everyone will pretend that everything is great if you don't open your lips
So we hold it in until we eventually vomit
Worrying about unlikely scenarios that defy all logic
Daughters with empowered ovaries always the target.

Being a daughter can be like an unfortunate trip
The free kind you get with a proof of purchase for your twentieth bag of chips
Including a small processing fee which is monetarily insignificant
From a sweepstakes you were selected
But the moment you arrive your dislike is instant
The promise of discovery and truthfulness is not apparent
Perplexed because everything is so different from the photos on the Internet
The receipt confirming what you were promised you should have kept
The accommodations are wrongly detailed in the pamphlet
But we smile and don't say shit
We unassumingly grin right through it
We suffer through it
We seem pleased when asked about it
If she seems pleased we will avoid any necessary topic
Like the disaster is welcomed and was sincerely meant
Acting like this dump is a bungalow in the tropics
When it comes to crafting phony realties

Our family can rock it!
Damn, we invented it!
I was taught to absorb the wrong while pretending to enjoy it
The truth?
Don't unload it
Keep it in the appropriate compartment
To avoid starting shit
Being a daughter is all about reading the fine print
Don't blink or you'll miss it
As I stare at my mother's signature on my birth certificate
I realize that I will never receive my human entitlement
I have the human right to live my own life
So, she's clearly negligent!
With her name etched on my certificate
All promises were voided upon issuing the document
I must have missed it
I learned that the souls of girls can be easily traded like magic
Mothers being named as the sole benefactor
Your job as a daughter becomes all about making her happier
Daughters used to trap or convince the man the mother is after
Or to create in the mother's life some new needed chapter
But that daughter will never be enough for what the mother is really after
Daughters harm themselves because they can't attack her
So you faintly hear her suffering behind her mother's laughter
Makes you wonder why she even had her.

### 222

A daughter born into a horrible relationship never meant to be saved

To their dysfunction and disrespect she was a little girl
enslaved
Following the unspoken rules of how a daughter is taught to
behave
Fantasizing about the freedom she hoped to attain one day
But every day of relief appears further and further away
She's seen too much now for those ancient Scriptures to any
longer persuade
Her mama is in church thanking the heavens for the day made
But when the daughter looks her way
All she can is the dishonesty, judgment, and intentional
provocation God clearly forbade
After 40 years in the wilderness I could no longer stay
For far too long she's had a say
She's determined to formations and strategies in a game she
doesn't even know how to play
I freed myself
Today is a new day
Now, I don't have to wrongly or blindly obey
For me I don't need you to pray
God granted me everything that I've ever wanted on that day
The day I finally got my mama out of my way.

<u>223</u>

Everything she was praying for
I was praying against
For me the kind of life I was directed towards could not persist
Her characteristics in me I wouldn't allow to exist
She's a mother doubling as a masochist
A narcissist mother in the purist
You'd also smell the manure once given a whiff

How could a real mother oppose a daughter's determination
not to be treated like shit?
I just don't get it.
Although smeared shit was always her favorite condiment
He'd give it and she expected me to just take it
Could you imagine that?
I refused to just embrace the ridiculousness in lieu of changing
it
And I wasn't afraid to call her out and specifically name it
I developed that inner strength on my own
So for my courageousness she can't take ANY credit
I cultivated it
And I alone did it
Her as a potential inspiration is wrong and defies all human
logic
Now, when it comes to discouragement
Her negative and destructive influence is the appropriate topic
When your mother is a narcissist you have to claim it
If you don't
She will surely steal it.

### 224

My life belonged to her and I wasn't even allowed to
customize it
Everything I said I didn't want she forced me to have it
I wasn't in control of my life even a little bit
Decades grown and I was still providing her with permission
slips
Even when I knew otherwise and was strong enough to
handle it
All decisions were based on how SHE felt about it
She wanted me to suffer like her and I can prove it

No matter the proof she'll lie and say she didn't do it
Daughters like us are so used to it
She wanted me to spend my life rowing when I preferred the cruise ship
I manage my money wisely and she's all about spending it
Asking her child for money, but swears she's an expert in all things economic
She's wasted it all and now has nothing show for it
When I hear her laughable justifications I become convinced that she should have become a comic
That dumb opinion and dogmatic insight is an imitation, but she still bought it
I can't even call it
And I am no longer afraid to admit it
A lying mouth with the bacteria infestation of five diseased dicks
Yeah, I said it and I mean it
And even though I proved to be right
She's still way too envious of my cleaver decision making to admit it
So be it.

### 225

I'm not bluffin'
I somehow made it into somethin'
And I did it all a sudden
When everyone thought I was bluffin'
I kept the written
I proved that I'm not hushin'
She's a mother who has created an impossible situation
False egos and lying is the first thing I now devour at the luncheons

For reasoning and honesty I am no longer searchin'
She know that her deception is hurtin'
I'm more suspicious of her than I am of the strangers lurkin'
Beware of the mother who only creates a daughter to loath a
life of pure strugglin'
And phony huggin'
Always hidden' somethin'
Daughter now understand why her father was running'
Trying to get out of a volatile situation, but the responsibility of
it all is tuggin'
He bought the wrong reality and now there is no returnin'
In front of me one or the other was steadily burnin'
The wrong way she's always rubbin'
A cruel and never-satisfied mother that always naggin'
Of evil she is the personification
The Bible she carries is just a prop
A sort of distraction
To keep them from seeing what's really lackin'
Every 3 seconds her lips are coveting or complaining and
smackin'
Trying her hardest to secure the daughter's worst reaction
Always judging and attackin'
She starts every disagreement and then pretend like she
doesn't know how it all happened
Constantly playing the poor victim
Always lyin'
But she better keep tryin'
Because I'm not buyin'
She and fear are bedfellows who love snugglin'
The minute I started earning money she began tuggin'
She takes what I make from working'
She kept my pocket hurtin'
Until I told her no more loanin'

I don't owe her somethin'
For doing little of nothin'
She owes me for all the sufferin'
She's responsible for the limitations and the cuffin'
Her hand is around your neck, but she'll blame him for the chokin'
But now I'm now ignorin'
When she reads this eye-opener she and her Terracotta Warriors will be stormin'
But this is what happened when for decades she ignored my warnin'
Now she learnin'
I don't give a shit if she's fumin'
The truth I'm tired of tuckin'
There will be no retraction
Poetic verses alleviate the suffocation
My words allow for greater emancipation
The daughter can relate to the commonality sensation
Daughter who feed off the wrong maternal stuff can cause constipation
Paralyzed tongues are afraid to announce our true mother-daughter situation
Over the years we've realized that our mothers are sick but we are the ones taking medication
And church is only worsening her delusions
It is very, very difficult conversing with a person obsessed with Revelation
You know
That kind of faux-Christian
Forget having an honest and sensible conversation
Talks are filled with her misguided dogma and unrealistic hallucinations

What a daughter says and feels receives no emotional or
mental penetration
So there had to be a separation
There was no way around her excommunication
She's been permanently removed from my delegation
Every photo of her is now marked for deletion
I realized that she'd never give me the deserved and sought
confirmation
So no more joint communion
I had the courage to end what warranted a much deserved
celebration
I clearly wasn't playin'
I've shoveled dirt on that emotional coffin
I'm just sayin'.

226

Don't get me wrong
Misfortune visits us all
I won't argue against the unfortunate predicaments
The possibility of avoidance is often irrelevant
But I have a beef with tirelessly ignoring it
Especially when you were the main participant
Pretending like it wasn't even significant
Like it's all hallucinogenic
Like my recall is all cinematic
The deception is making me asthmatic
Sending me into a panic
You lie even when honesty is demanded
Blood loyalty ain't even respected
Truthfulness is always negated
I know even though you'll never say it
A mother who can't be trusted

Afraid to own it?
So I wrote it
Now everyone knows it
I own my shit
And I ain't hardly perfect
But when it comes to the truth
I'm worth it
It is easier to forgive when you acknowledge all of it
Until you can face it
To the idea of forgiveness I will remain intolerant.

### 227

Your mother should have acknowledged and apologized
Your disgust and dismay should not come as a surprise
"I'm sorry for anything that you think I MAY have done," she
said
That woman is sick in the head!
That lame and phony comment hardly sufficient
And she surly knows it
The daughters who back you have already said it
A real apology is owed
You've already confessed what you definitively know
How much more proof could a daughter possibly show?
You are even certain of her clandestine role
But you sit silently shaking your head as she puts on her self-
righteous robe
The one she obviously stole
Because she wouldn't have it in her possession if honor and
truthfulness was the goal
For the next ten minutes she starts wailing about Jesus
That's her way of circumventing all of her crimes and treasons
The Bible helps her devise ridiculous scenarios and reasons

Lord, here we go!
I have to listen to her pretend not to know anything about it
She's ready to deem every memory insignificant
Denial for her is an epidemic
Lying is just intrinsic
I know you are sick of her shit
I understand why you will no longer put up with it
It's crystal clear to me
I totally get it.

228

Every time I think I'm done
Writing and reflecting on something else she's shamefully
done
All over again I become undone
Mothers like that should not be allowed to breed
Before birthing a daughter a simple psychological evaluation
should be in need
Someway to predict the likelihood of her future maternal
misdeeds
And to preliminarily detect her jealousy for her own seed
When you receive a mother that damaged
A daughter can spend a lifetime trying to break free from her
oppressive standards
But now I have the advantage!
The life she seized and once controlled
Now I manage!
I reclaimed what she stole
The life I live now is all my own.

229

He can't rub two nickels together

Yet you believed that his long-time mistress was his maid?
Uh, what, wait?
That's a known lie that you should be embarrassed to even repeat or say
Even your teenage daughter knew it wasn't that way
But cluelessness and denial are your forte
A few hundred for his rent is all he had to pay
And that's his maid you say?
Are you even listening to yourself today?
You even act like he didn't create an entirely different family from back in the day
We aren't the only ones with his last name
He been running game
And your dismissal of reality has gotten so obvious it's a shame
Your kind of deniability is just insane
And the bullshit you recycle I can't even wade
The lies you two would constantly trade
He's played by the same playbook yet you claim to not know about the plays
But I figured it out at eight!
So how'd you not know what move he'd make?
As a child I could anticipate every action without mistake
Why are you still so confused and late?
Lying won't get you into those pearly gates
Especially when it the devil with whom you lay
You'd suffer through every humiliation just for him to stay
As a woman it shamed me to see you obey
To never have the courage to move away
A promise of rent, a pension, and some miniscule spending money was always enough to stay
It was sickening watching the games you two would play

You are still married to a man who you haven't seen since my 20ᵗʰ birthday
How's that okay?
A weak woman in every way
I said I'd pay for the divorce and you still
He lives with his "maid" and you still won't walk away
Brandishing your defunct wedding ring to this very day
What does that say?
Even his visits to the swingers clubs when I was little were okay
You should have known because I was plain as day

Religion and judgment proved to be your preferred way
You wouldn't stickup for yourself
So constantly chastising me became okay
The way you'd cope each day
Teaching your daughter that women are mandated to endure abuse your actions would say
You are slated to be the ancestor that I'd grow to despise one day
I realize now that you can't be cured and you will never change
I never saw a hand held, hug, a kiss, a kind word exchanged
Not even an embrace
But he and I don't live that way
I don't reenact your mistakes
Our joy and happiness is at stake

It's hard for others to imagine a home where genuine love never took place
The seemingly good times never outweighed
The burden of being your daughter became too much to take

An environment where fake obligations triumph over sincerity
was always commonplace
That I chose to erase
You never had a peaceful or happy expression on your face
Everything had a bitter taste
Oh, what a waste
Of a life that could have justified occupation of my space
When your mother is your enemy a girl runs at a different kind
of race
Always giving up first place
My trophy she'd always take
Like she actually ran the race
It was like that every day.

### 230

Daughters like us are marathon runners who have never
actually trained
But we come in first place all the same
We will lay in any bed we have made
We're get back on course no matter how far we've strayed
We trust our intuition and wisdom when we think we're being
played
The masculine disrespect and abuse she condones
We won't let stay
We don't subscribe the generational ordinance of "obey"
We aren't made that way
We speak to truth about the obstacles in our way
We can't be silenced by a new a purse and a pair of designer
shades
Materialism won't make reality go away
No bribe will overshadow the disrespect and make us stay
We take our kids and we get the hell away

We don't repeat the lies he wants us to believe or say
We don't need anyone to rescue us when we cry mayday
We don't teach our daughters that what is wrong is actually okay
We teach them to demand more and never suppress what she may need to say
When his mistress calls the house we won't act like that behavior is okay
She's in the front seat of his car in our driveway
He's with his newest mistress and the woman of the house ain't got shit to say
Despite the humiliation the mother will stay
I swore I'd never let you make me that way
I'm so glad I got away.

## 231

Daughters like us make decisions many adult children never have to make
So I admire you and respect any decision path that you may take
It's not easy and I surely can relate
And I congratulate you on being awake
I commend you on being real while surrounded by the fake
Your awareness of yourself certifies what you will and will not take
For your sanity's sake
On being happy you decided to no longer wait
Your tenacity I surely appreciate
I'm amazed at your ability to reject her assigned fate
Kudos to you for not making her same life mistakes
And when your peacefulness and happiness were at stake

You bravely banished her to the outside of our soul's security
gate
Let'em hate.

### 232

I'm too far gone
I've bought every book about her devious-ass on Amazon
I had to sound the alarm
Before the next generation of daughters are born
It's time they learn
We won't wait forever for our turn.
For me
Only writing quits the storm
Beware of a daughter scorned.

### 233

She asks if I'm sure
She wants to ignore medicine and solely seek God for the
cure
Either or makes it all difficult to endure
Both combined will seemingly ensure
There are too many dead prayers for her ideology to seem
pure
Her two cents and crazy religious talk causes me to be
insecure
Her dogmatic stance is less inspiring and smells more like
manure
Removing her from the situation would be an improvement I'm
sure
The exclusion of her two-cent is the secret cure
You alone own your body

She can't grant any unauthorized visits or preapproved tours.

## 234

When she turned forty
She knew heads would roll
But she didn't expect her mother to be the first cranium on the pole
That she surely didn't know
But that's how life goes
Years of frustrations, anger, and undisguised observations came flooding out
The damaged adult daughters out there know exactly what I'm talking about
Only more lies and Jesus references are coming from her mouth
You finally let it out
And you said what is known but no one is willing to talk about
You finally have the courage to call that witch out
And you're proud of yourself for not sitting the confrontation out
You are an adult now and no longer the child who is without
You finally figured her evil scheme out
You realized that she doesn't know what the hell she's talking about
And you can't trust ANYTHING out of her mouth
Her coldness causes the birds in your yard to immediately fly south
Liars like her must to shout
She thinks that it keeps you from figuring her out
And she's powerless but pretends to have some type of ordained clout
What the hell is she talking about?

But you aren't 12 years old anymore and sadly sitting on her couch
She's in your home instigating a new idiotic bout
And is only muttering a series of incoherent biblical shouts
Only confirming that you don't know what the hell she's talking about
She was surprised that you took that courageous route
You finally called that liar out!
Now she knows that you know what she's REALLY all about
She is guilty of everything you said and I'd be happy to vouch
Sitting there looking baffled and offended on your damn couch
You finally got her and her and her bullshit the fuck out!
Now, that's what I'm talking about!
That's something that you have the right to be delighted about
She had you down
But you were never out.

235

For as long as you can remember she's told you that the end was near
Yet we are the daughters who have survived her campaign of daily fear.

And despite her curses of doom we're still here
So our admissions to other struggling daughters only makes our purpose more clear.

Her renewed cycle of last days begins anew every single New Year
And each January 1st she becomes more jealous of your ability to reappear.

Her inability to be loving and sincere hasn't affected your
happiness and cheer
She claims to be God's spokesperson even though
encouragement isn't something that you ever hear.

She's losing so she ramps up her utilization of judgmental fear
To ideas of religious punishment and spiritual retribution she
loves to adhere.

So, if there's one thing I could tell you, oh, Daughter Dear
Continue to courageously progress while always keeping her
negativity and doom-day beliefs in the rear.

### 236

I did it on my terms
In my house
With my voice
With my own strength
With my own audacity
Without any tears
I told you that I didn't trust you
I told you that you are the biggest liar in the world
How could everything be deniable?
How is it that you are NEVER liable?
How is it that you are NEVER responsible?
Why aren't you EVER accountable?
Nothing that you say is EVER credible
With you the truth is NEVER retrievable
Religion being used to hide the noticeable
Very little that you say is even truly believable
I fully stand by my awareness and declaration of your lies
Christian by day and deceiver by night

You know you ain't right
They may say I'm disrespectful
But you were in my house
In my domain I'm all powerful
In here my husband and I have no rivals
We are both sane and you're the only psycho
Don't come in here with your judgmental nature trying to screw-up my solitude
You were begging to feel my attitude
This house was peaceful until you purposely fucked-up the whole mood
Coming in here criticizing and disrespecting like somebody owes you
But now you know
For years you've been hitting far below
You always bring me back when I try to forgive and let go
And now everyone who bought your phony act will know
You ain't never been a real mother to me
All that shit was just for show
I'm just confessing what you and I both know.

## 237

Being raised by two compulsive liars is like being raised by wolves
Centaurs are ever present but only you see the hooves
The evidence of unicorns will likely provide more proof
Honest comments vanish before there is in any evidence of poof
The myth of Bigfoot is more closely affiliated with the truth
Of a loving and real family we're only a spoof
Like a *Few Good Men* we can't handle the truth
How can they all be so aloof?

Out of six only two of us will tie together all the evasive and
scheming clues
Smoke and mirrors
That's what we're used to
Past lies can also determine the future too
Deceitfulness is always encouraged when candidness simply
won't do.

### 238

She rules through fear and emotional abuse
Daughters like us are always misused
We fight back, but what's the use?
Her countless demands make it impossible to hit snooze
She wants you convinced that your daddy is to blame and he's
the only issue
But more tears have been shed over your mother than him in
those tissues
Don't expect understanding or empathy from those who refuse
to acknowledge the obvious clues
You need to start implementing your own daughter protection
rules
Round your neck is your inherited noose
Who will you choose?

### 239

Another promise broken
Here and there are tiny assured tokens
In sincere and unfulfilled promises she's always making
Every unbelievable lie is for the taking
Happiness she's always stealing
Claiming to have been heavenly selected to do God's bidding

Then you realize that the mother you want is never coming
Like your father she's always bluffing
When it comes to criticism she's always talking
Her redelivery of the same falsehoods is no longer working
What "she's going to do" she's always evoking
But you once again see absolutely nothing
So fantastical her illusions she must be smoking
With her madness I will no longer be eloping
Her Terracotta Warriors must now do her biding
Seeing is believing.

### 240

She's pretends to be religious
But she ain't prestigious
She's delirious
So malicious
The emotional calculus
Oh, so callus
Everything is bogus
But now she's powerless
I've earned this
And I won't miss.

### 241

Delusions of Grandeur
Never side with the liar
Over the frankness and honesty of the daughter
She's a girl who can't try any harder

There will never be a reconciliation
There's been too much rejection

She can say that she doesn't have a mother without
absolutely no hesitation

Once the world hears her side
And she no longer has to hide
Or with those dumb-ass rules cease to abide
The mother will surely lie
No fake tears will fall from her eyes
She will deny, deny, deny
And she'll use Jesus and every book of the Bible as her alibi
Transparency she would never try
It was either she or I
And she knows why.

## 242

You're not the troublemaker
She's the real evildoer and faker
She's selling the same bullshit, but you won't be a taker
Move a thousand of miles away and you still can't shake her
You've learned not to trust anyone who works for her
Similar DNA can place a person under her thumb
So tired of trying to outrun
Too tired of trying to be the good and obedient daughter
Tired of forgiving each time you're left at the alter
But over YOUR life YOU are the author
It's too much of an effort to call when you really rather not
bother
You will NEVER be able to please your selfish and faux-
religious mother
You've learned not to bother
Why should you suffer?
She has your Terracotta Warrior brothers

Always wishing she was something other
God bless the daughters of horrid and psycho mothers
She tried harder
But we wouldn't let them take us under.

## 243

Never allow her to convince you that it is not okay to claim
Give your ailment or whatever you are battling name
Avoidance and denying can appear the same
It's okay to recognize and acknowledge the storms when it
rains
Don't sidestep the things that you know aren't okay
Don't pretend like you don't have something to say
You can't defeat what you don't divulge today
That's a sure way to quickly end the game
Claim it all I say
Ignoring its existence won't make it go away
What's hidden still exists despite all of her encouraged
dismissals and delays
Don't let her tell you that it must be this or that way
How could your honesty and determination not be God's way?
It is okay to say
It's alight to claim
Call it by its name
Don't allow HER dogma to get in YOUR way
What kind of sense does that make?
What you don't claim today
You will have to accept one day
You will eventually have to face what you have long avoided
anyway
Be careful of who you blindly obey
Negation won't force it anyway
Acceptance is okay
The truth cannot be further delayed
To yourself there is a psychological and emotional debt that
must be paid
Within you the nameless still remains
Ignoring the existence will drive you insane

The internal conflict will cause an emotional and spiritual strain
Learn to live without absorbing her misplaced shame
You aren't in control of everything and not everything you can tame
Denial kept her from fighting what forever lingered and stayed
No growth
No improvement
She's still the same
Daughter, give it a name
Live without shame
Or be the one to blame.

## 244

A distant daughter from a far-off land
But we are a lot alike from where I stand
Similar expectations and unfair sexist demands
What is held back from her is given freely to the man
Her life only revolves around his plans
Mothers tell us that that's what God commands
But we seem to be the only one who gives a damn
Down our throats the rules and assumptions they constantly ram
What's hard for Suzie is easy for Sam.

## 245

They'll say you're being too hard on her
But you haven't even mentioned half the scars
It's always all about her
And never about you
Never concerned about your experiences
No one seems to care about what you been through
She's never been honest or told a single truth
Yet you still put up with her emotional abuse

They should be ashamed of themselves
And you should be proud of you
You did what none of them had the guts or courage to do
They're still stuck in her cesspool of toxicity
But you made it out and through.
Girl, good for you!


## 246

Christina Aguilera's, *Fighter*
That song reminds of my relationship with my mother
And my father.

We're accused of being "too grown"
When young girls like us want it known
Sexism and misogyny
I felt it more by her than men.

I know what it is like to be under constant sexist and
misogynistic attack
I see her in me today and even when I look back
Huh, imagine that.

## 247

The situation is volatile
The circumstances are hostile
My questions I've compiled
As far back as being a child
She'll say that my imagination is wild
But I remembered accurately all the while
To deflect she'll try to put me on trial

The lies behind that fake-ass smile
I won't be liable
When she denies being responsible
When she tries to avoid being negligible
Anything is probable
Her excuses will be laughable
To her all of my evidence is deniable
My furry is ignitable
Expecting honesty from the unstable
I have finally turned the tables
I've finally addressed the cradle
Before I was unable
But the weak daughter is now able
No more fables.


## 248


First instinct is to lead her to the kitchen
Trying to make you as subservient as her is the only mission
Everything is based on tradition
But adult daughters everywhere are forcing an intermission
We are changing our thinkin'
On that star we're no longer wishin'
Our mothers don't have the right to force our decisions
Families everywhere need an intervention
Adult daughters are disagreeing with that perception
There needs to be some way to protect daughters from those
sexist interpretations
Mothers not allowing daughters not given right to decent and
offer objection
What our mothers force on us is often met with silent
repudiation
But we are told our happiness isn't worth the mention
Doing it our way is always met with rejection

There is an intentional effort to dismiss our disrespect our
selection
Adult daughters are forced into difficult and disadvantageous
situations
And our mothers can never be trusted with fair consultation
All over the world mothers play pimps and decide who is
suitable for layin'
His suitability is tied to what he's payin'.

The "provider" title to her is the ultimate sensation
As long as he can "provide" daughters are taught to ignore
love and compassion
His "provider" status dictates our decision
These ideals place daughters in a lose-lose situation.

The ideal husband is based on her
Her recommendation
Her evaluation
He determination
I'm so glad I didn't listen!
Not for you, but for her gratification
Maybe your husband will improve her situation
Now she has two incomes available to get her out of her many
financial situations
She should have been the one enduring the consummation.

Mothers often determine what man leaves and which one is
staying
Never closely observing the image of women that they are
portraying
They look at the women over there and condemn in unison
But over here family bullying is used on daughters to influence
their decisions
Mothers even involved the other sibling in the collision
We marry folks based on our mother's preferences and
instigations
It's a screwed-up situation
What the daughter wants or doesn't want is HER decision
For an independent woman there is often no provision
Mothers like mine hate daughters with self-determination

Especially since ruining them has been the mother's primary concentration.

But I'm not stressin'
The mistreatment of women in certain families all over the world is quite displeasin'
A patriarchal system designed to ignore the legions
Designed to take away a daughter's right to reason
An oppression of the gender based on interpretations of a biased religion
Nations away we can't understand why they aren't listenin'
But mothers over here are using their homes to also deny the rights of the female citizen
The sexism and cruelty of a mother also incarcerates daughters within a sort of prison
Our very right to happiness and to live our own lives our mothers are seizin'
The honesty shared by the daughter no one is believin'
In our homes there is a hidden and urgent mother-daughter tension
But since it isn't about men or boys they fail to mention
It doesn't receive the necessary attention
Daughters forced to uphold and perpetuate antiquated and draconian systems
Mothers encouraging daughters to endure and stay in dangerous relationships and situations
All so the mother can collect on the misfortune
But we no longer need your permission
We will make our own decisions
Respect it and listen
These daughters are on a mission.

249

She thanks God everyday
That she had the courage to finally have her say
To speak up for the grown daughters who are too afraid

Years of frustration and legitimate gripes sprawled out on a page
Decades of unspoken rage
The damage that she couldn't allow to contaminate and stay
She knew that from the motherhood she experienced she's have to stray
Is she wanted the family she created to be free
She always knew she'd have to cut off the dead branches from her growing tree
She found the courage to recount the evidence of the maternal strange
They've asked her not to perform the secret on the world stage
But the astronomical debt of concealment she will no longer pay
She could no longer look away
She is offering a needed voice to what has already been made
She has no reverence for what the superstitious and the faux-family may say
Daughters not allowed to be honest about their reality
While she defames and lies against us everyday
If you have good stories to tell daughters are permitted to regurgitate the memories
But any unpleasant truths we are not allowed to speak
Her life will be liver her way
Within these pages those adult daughters of those mothers finally have a place.

250

I won't say it if I can't live it
I won't fuel it if I can't feel it
I know I was taught the opposite

I even married who she wanted
A bad marriage will try to ruin you won't it?
Don't make me say it
Respect?
I now demand it
I require it
It's now a primary requirement
And if of our mothers can't give it
The maternal figures in our life will give it
What isn't you can't make it
With other hurt adult daughters
Always remember to share it
Your story
Don't neglect it
Don't repudiate it
And where you're headed
She can't stop it
Best believe it.

## 251

Thank you for sharing your art
You taught me that it is okay to recognize what emotionally
rips me apart
This song gave me the courage to finally start
And to finally share my hidden poetic art
I have the courage to write because of you
And in particular,
This song affirmed for me that my writings were okay to share
and do
Mistakes and all I'm sending to you
I just want the world to know my truth
And music have helped me to make it through

And an optimistic Romero Britto painting or two.


Mondo Grosso featuring Amel Larrieux,
*Now You Know Better*
That's the song of my life and speaks my truth
Amel sings my life to the letter
Reminding me that time and experience work in unison to
make it better
And I want the daughters and sons to hear her
Even to this day when I hear that song I still cry
The tears begin to flow when I hear that profound lullaby
When the other daughters like me hear it they'll know why
That song speaks to me and musically captures my entire life
When I decided to no longer blindly follow
That song was my light
And it helped me to remain strong and fight
Because I knew that Mondo and Amel knew I was right
And that song has impacted my life
And it empowered me to ultimately get it right
Those lyrics explain perfectly what being in my skin is like
You sung of my type
You verbalized every thought and emotion I had secluded
inside
You musically reveled what I would insecurely hide.


Then there is Kid Cudi's, *Pursuit of Happiness*
There is little better than it
When I hear it I'm happy and content
Knowing that Kid Cudi feels me
And to Duncan Sheik's, *Barely Breathing*, I sing every line
It is another favorite of mine

And I'm so grateful for Kelis' mastery and for blessing me with
*Trilogy* / *Bossy* / *Till The Wheels Fall Off* / *Goodbyes* / *Fuck
Them Bitches* / *Circus* / *Aww Shit* / *Have A Nice Day* / *Like
You* / Mars / *Appreciate Me* / *Lil Star* / *Handful* / *Caught Out
There* / *Young Ghetto Children* / *Game Show* / Fresh N' New
To this day her many songs help me to shine
She's been there through every climb
Her music helps me to clear my mind
And Stevie Wonder's, *Innervisions* album has helped me feel
fine
And Undisputed Truth's, *Smiling Faces* chronicle my truth in
every line
They ain't never lied!
While the Robert Glasper Experiment's *Black Radio Volume 1*
and *Black Radio Volume 2* are so, so super, super dope!
And Emeli Sandé's *Somebody Else* , from *Black Radio
Volume 2*, always gets my vote.
From front to back both albums I can quote
Thank you for every word inspired sung and every word and
melody wrote and instrument note.

And Norah Jones', *Let It Ride,* from *Black Radio 2* helps me to
clear the day's emotional smoke
And I feel Kendrick in my soul.
And to me the O'Jays *Backstabbers* song has always spoke
And Frank Sinatra's, *My Way* is always on my mind
And Gladys Knight and the Pips, *Best Thing That Ever
Happened To* Me is for the husband always on my side
And like Dwele's Old Lovers we gonna ride for life.
And Anita Baker 's *Angel* will always be a favorite of mine.
And Incognitos *True To Myself* will always be an anthem of
mine
And Junip's, *Line of Fire* is an awesome musical find

And Phonte's, *Who Loves You More* featuring Eric Roberson
speaks the truth every damn time!
I swear Phonte's music can touch and save lives!
He definitely has improved mine
And my husband co-signs.


And Oddisee's song, *Book Covers* is beyond true
And *Wide Open Spaces* by the Dixie Chicks helped me to do
what I had to do
And I was *Brave* and I *Roar*ed like Sarah and Katy said
And as DJ Quik's *Quik Groove* plays faintly in my head
I had an emotional garage sell and I've cleaned out everything
dead
As always, I left every single error in this book because my
perfectionism almost left me for dead
And by leaving mistakes visible, for all to see, it helps me to
get my mother's unrelentless perfectionism demands out of
my head
And instead of obsessing over them I decide to let them stand
I decided to lay them bare in vulnerability instead
Against the pro perfectionism and anti-vulnerability thoughts
she placed into my head
And although The Black Cat Daughters are discussing what
our mothers did
Know that even though we are acknowledging our truths
We are still moving ahead
Sorry that when you needed a mother
You got her instead
And instead of good things about you she put the worst into
your head
But don't you be scared,
Daughter, hold my hand instead.

## 252

Consider this work of art to be a poetic documentary
All about adult daughters who suffer like you and me
In her, evil is masqueraded as a "loving mommy"
But that ain't hardly our reality
That ain't what we see
More than anyone we have ever known she lacks the most
loyalty
She has never lived honestly
But swears she's the nearest to the divinity
Witch, please!
She ain't really praying for you when she on her knees
She's begging not to reap the repercussions from her
mammoth evil deeds
She's always, always lying
And for the truth you will always be waiting
Because it ain't never-ever coming
Honesty ain't never-ever happening
And everything she didn't rightfully earn she's surely taking
Credit for your hard work and accomplishments she's
ALWAYS claiming
Even though she did very, very little to nothing
Her very presence is a dishonest and rude awakening
And the constant fighting
Oh, it's just all so very, very tiring
Evil mothers ain't worth admiring
With the devil and not God she's surely conspiring
That faux-Christian "mother" needs to go into permanent
hiding
Because she knows the guidelines for a good mother
But that demonic spirit ain't abiding.

## 253

I call her faux-Godly
Around my misfortunes my shady-ass "mother" likes to party
Pretending to be so pious and saintly
Yet, about me she is always lying and gossiping

She isn't at all who she claims to the world to be
Her morally deficient minions recite her dishonest propaganda
exactly
Men with no tongues are all she's known for creating
Relaying her false bullshit is the only thing they can do
effectively
And I'm not afraid to say it if you ask me
And her own siblings act as if hatefulness and jealousy is
sisterly
The way that they treat each other is the way she treats me
Dishonest and phony
Can't call yourself a "mother" when honesty and love for your
daughter is always missing
Stop pretending.

### 254

How dare you?
Never underestimate what an infuriated, mistreated, and
critically judged daughter will do
I've always tried to accept and love you
Despite you
Why couldn't you?
I even stomached your constant and compulsive lying too
I tried even when I knew you weren't telling the whole truth
Always waiting in vain for some honesty or some kind of
psychological breakthrough in you
After forty years I knew
That nothing honest would ever come through you
And every single time I'd stupidly forgive you
Only to watch you reoffend and devise a new lie or dramatic
issue
Why is everything always about you, you, you?
Daughters are never of any concern to cruel and evil mothers
like you
But we matter too
Even if not to you
And it is because of you
That I never believe that a liar is telling me the truth
Especially not a faux-Christian like you

It's so odd how easily deception flows through you
So "saintly," but has never put God to any good use
To condemn and curse your own daughter is all you have ever
used God to do
It is a curse for a daughter to be born to a mother like you
You should have just had the abortion you said my father
wanted you to have if this is what you'd do
Full of envy, cruelty, physical and even emotional abuse
They say you can't give to me what your own parents never
gave to you
But I know that shit ain't true
Just look at me and look at you
Choices and truth is all it boils down to
I'm able to give to other adult daughters despite what you
refused to do
Even after all the many, many times I told you
I managed to get my life right all without you
Consider my books as living proof
That adult daughters like me really don't need evil-ass
mothers like you
Everything you tried to sabotage
Watch us do.

## 255

Adult daughters, expect to see a whole lot of me in you
Forecast nodding your head in agreement while reading our
shared truths
Through the cruelty of your own mother
You'll surely see mine too.

Our mothers have been allowed for far too long to play their
sick manipulative games
And they work religiously to stifle and discourage our attempts
to improve our situations and demand change
And ending up like them would only make us miserable and
ashamed
So, over our own lives we have decided to exclusively reign
Mothers like ours are a damn shame.

She isn't who she portrays to be
She pretends to be so caring
But we've personally witnessed her secret jealousy
The envy they refuse to acknowledge we always see
She's envious of the fact that her daughter's life doesn't
resemble her own tragedy
Her daughter is independent, self-reliant and tremendously
happy
Something her mother never really wanted her to be
She raised her under the cloud of dependency
To always think of them but never consider me
Oh, she only taught religious and oppressive fallacies
The good in life her mean mother never wanted her to see
But there is no sense in worrying
Daughters, let's drop the emotional baggage we've been
carrying
Stop hauling her shame and her projecting
Her constant insults we are always handling
For simple respect we are always battling
Face it
She'll never-ever be loving
She'll never-ever be understanding
And she ain't changing
Against what is real daughters must stop wrestling
Stop fighting
The evil and un-motherly crap she's done leaves us gasping
Every cruel statement by her we're continuously interpreting
Her negativity we are absorbing
Every slight out of her mouth we are dissecting
Her chastisements we are constantly internalizing
Having a mother like that is truly traumatizing
And when we walk away
Her low-integrity genetic minions start whining
Our ability to confront our toxic mother-daughter relationships
will prove to be life defining
With yourself are you complying?
Stop compromising
For her authorization just stop freakin' trying

Start never-minding
Afraid to say what needs to be said because of her chiding
I know her meanness and criticalness can be blinding
With your needs she will never, never begin complying
She'd much rather leave you upset and crying
How many more lies and deceptions will you be buying?
With certain people you just have to stop trying
That's something I'm finally realizing.

## 257

If you read carefully you'll hear me speak
If you listen carefully you may even hear my words over J
Dilla's Fall In Love beat
When it comes to poetry
Some daughters call me the greatest of all time
The G.O.A.T. they say, but I don't mind
I'm just a messenger gifted by the divine
To move forward and to continue to help adult daughters find
their shine
Daughters like us have to constantly rewind
Confronting your damaging mother issues will help you from
taking that drink and doing that line
Oh, oh, how they blame the emotionally absent fathers every
damn time
And few fathers were as effed'up as mine
Effed'up fathers serve life
But effed'up mothers never have to do any time
They tell us to let it go by-and-by
As she ushers in your decline
Society refuses to acknowledge that mean and evil mothers
actually do the worst crimes
She'll eff'up her daughters and everyone turns a blind eye
Just being called a "mother" allows them to cross every line
But why?
I believe in the equality of the sexes so why can't cruel
mothers also fry?
Maybe it ain't the father's fault this time
Why is the father always blamed for ruining a daughter's life?
Adult daughter, when you are silent you're lying

She's only doing what you're allowing
And no one believes us because she's so "kind" and so
"charming"
That kind of stoic evil should be alarming.

## 258

Today, I feel invincible!
Whatever you have to dismissively say isn't that critical
Without truthfulness, you really can't have any other valuable
principles
Why do you make MY individuality and MY beliefs your damn
issue?
Everything that comes out of your mouth is as dubious as a
minstrel
Your lack of real love and support for your own daughter is the
real issue.

Why you are the way that you are, I'll never know
Every time I expect honesty, the truth always ends up being a
no-show
And I become exhausted from averting all of your low blows
Wherever you're headed, I already know
That's NOT the way I should go
One day you too will reap the underhandedness and
deception that you love to sow
When it comes to being evil you're a pro.

## 259

It's funny how they don't believe you
Everyone underestimates what we've been through
Only those who truly know and love you
Honestly believe you
Her crimes are never committed in front of people
So when that indolent alibi is stated,
I have a real issue.

Especially since you, not them, was the one crying into the
boxes tissues

Adult daughter, we stand with you
Even your siblings will try to discredit your story too
Daughter, I feel you
Don't let your haters and doubters dictate what you will or won't do
It ain't up to them
It's up to you
It's funny how contagious amnesia is when it comes to you
Those who should know act as if they don't have clue.

But don't let their repudiation or cruelty affect you
Don't be swayed by fools
They may never understand that your honesty is the only morally required proof
And when it comes to real motherhood that wicked woman is just a spoof
So, I want you to know that the daughters stand with you
Wherever your story takes you
That is the avenue you should pursue
The truth only requires confirmation from you
And when your scars are internal,
How do we submit into evidence our internal proof?
Let your shady-ass family members act aloof
But know that we got you!
We are the adult daughters who suffer through it to
When you've truthfully said and done all you can do,
Just send your truth deniers a heartfelt and sincere, "fuck you!"
Because that's what I do.

### 260

If you believe what my mother says to be true
I have 19 lilac unicorns and 74 purple elephants to show you.

She's a phony goodie-two-shoes
She has everyone fooled except for me and you
She wants respect but loves to disrespect and lie to you.

Always having to cater to that mean witch

But she never returns the favor when the roles are switched.

Seeing and hearing real mothers love their daughters is
always refreshingly foreign to me
It's something that I have a hard time relating.

Because that positive mother-daughter relationship didn't
happen to me
My mother has always been my nemesis and my staunch
maternal enemy.

Everything is about fulfilling her needs while trying to ignore
her cruelty
And what she wants and thinks she falsely deserves I was
always providing.

Every holiday and birthday I'm giving thoughtful and sincere
gifts
While she walking around her apartment looking to hand me
some horrible re-gift.

And most years I get nothing
I never receive what she says was ordered and is coming
She's lying.

Maybe occasionally a birthday gift card or something
But that's after decades and decades of practically nothing.

Almost every word out of her mouth is a lie
But loves being the first one in church to testify.

"The older you get the more like me you become," she once
stupidly said
That was confirmation for me that she is officially sick in the
head.

Because becoming anything like her as a woman has always
been my worst fear
So her way of living, thinking, and depending I've worked hard
to steer clear.

But she has always tried to force me to be her clone
And I told her that I have the right to not go along.

She argumentatively disagreed
And said that I HAD to be whom she raised me to be
Well, she raised me to be a liar and to never live honestly.

But if I had become the pathetic woman she raised me to be
I'd be miserable, oppressed, and like her, clearly unhappy.

I wouldn't have anything
Nothing more than mere surviving and nothing reflective of
true living
Anything more, she felt that I wasn't deserving.

She raised me to be always be subservient to a man
She taught me that a woman didn't have the right to be happy
and make demands.

Her way of existing didn't fit anywhere within my plans
And her realm of purposely inflicted wounds and intentional
struggle I refused to land.

Me replicating her faux-religious, fake, loveless, insincere, and
unhappy life would be wrong
Unlike her, I am not a weak woman who is afraid to stand
alone.

So don't believe anything she's said or claims to have shown
Only those with integrity and common sense refuse to go
along
Her dumb minions may buy her perpetual bullshit
But I'm gone!

### 261

Daughter, don't allow her to make you feel ashamed
Don't live in your mother's failures nor her secret shame
Daughter, you have a totally different destiny and name

Regardless of what she may or may not say
She ain't rooting for you to succeed no way
You have the human right to live YOUR life YOUR way
Never trust a mother who lies and uses dogma to intimidate
you day after day
The sad and pathetic life your mother lives today
Is centered on the horrible decisions she tried to force you to
make yesterday
And her minions are enablers who assist her in getting in her
own way
The only way to win championships and rings in life is to never
run her losing plays
I realized that on that day
She only has herself to blame
She's jealous of you because you had the courage to speak
and lay claim
You'll say it in front of your "family" and you will call it out by
name
Unlike everyone else
You ain't afraid
She's envious because you got out, but she's still existing in
that pain
Girl, stop taking advice about winning from mothers who've
never won a game
If you listen to her, you lame!
Always be suspicious when a mother tries to lead you back
that wrong way
Keep it extremely short and don't you stay
You can spot her misguided followers because they're likely in
the same delusional place
For weak folks, she keeps in her cold heart a special space
Her minions sit at the narcissist's feet with the umbilical cord
still attached while drinking breast milk every day
Listen carefully
Because they'll always, always repeat what you heard your
shady-ass "mama" say
Run, don't walk the other away
She'll get hers one day
"And it couldn't have happened to a more deserving person,"
we will gladly say.

Who would want that kind of criticalness around? Her
negativity deliberately aims to bring you down.

I think she secretly wants you to stumble and fail,
She calls herself your mother, but she makes it hard to tell.
She treats you as if your decisions are always flawed and your
wisdom is somehow frail,
She pretends to be so ultra-holy and loving
But whenever you truly need her she never supports and
always bails.

You have learned to never revere or drink from her toxic faux-
maternal well,
And you now realize that her words aren't as coveted as the
Holy Grail.

You are the daughter of a synthetic mother and you have a
unique story to tell,
I know how many days and nights you have suffered and
wailed.

Your relationship with her has clearly grown nightmarish,
moldy, and irrefutably stale,
She can't understand or hear you even when you yell.

She is entangled in the judging and the silent critiquing that
she does so very well,
Constantly searching for every teeny-weeny imperfection on
your exterior shell.

Under her intimidation, do not let your voice or boldness quell,
The minute she starts faultfinding, you should be prepared to
bail.

And as the anger in you starts to swell,
Remember that you are not alone and I understand your
situation very, very well.

Say it anyway,
It's your truth to tell.

## 263

The longer you put up with it,
The more her negative energy will infect and inhabit.

The fear you once had you no longer have it,
She even found a deceptive way to make that unconvincing
hoax disappear like magic!

She loves making her freezer-burned-cold-heart appear
delicate,
All the while hating on you for defeating it,
She's envious because despite her negativity and judgment,
You still amazingly achieved it.

She is still getting away with the same crap she pulled
yesterday today!
She uses the same manipulative strategies to try to intimidate
you into doing it her way.

When her hypocrisy continues to fuel your inattention and
delay,
She takes hell and the Bible out for a play date.

She hasn't matured or worked to improve her life and your
relationship a single bit,
And she thinks that all of your mother-daughter gripes are
insignificant and irrelevant.

To you she's never been truly caring or honestly sympathetic,
She'll never get.

You two don't share the mutual love expected through a
common ancestry,
When it should be about you she makes it all about me, me,
me.

Who in the hell does she think she is?
Still trying to exert her tyranny over an adult daughter who is
clearly no longer her maid...I mean kid.

She is clearly demented and confused,
The maternal influence she once had, she willfully and
wrongly misused.

Like you, I have nothing else to say or even prove,
Every lie she tells leaves you more and more perturbed and
confused.

So now, you must make your own damn rules!
You are free to make independent decisions that she can't
permit or disapprove.
Evaluate your unique circumstances and you freely choose,
Whatever happens next is completely up to you.

It's time to make your own moves,
When it comes to your peace of mind and happiness,
There's no way you can lose.

Your obligation to yourself you must never undo,
I know you've been lied to,
But I strongly encourage you,
Work to move past the deceptions you are powerless to undo.

If given the opportunity she'd try to destroy that too,
You already know what you must do,
It's time to make self-preservation paramount for you.

### 264

I refuse to allow her to have any more control in my life,
To me, she has never been the mothering type.

It's so hard to pretend to be overjoyed,
Especially when you recognize that you have that maternal
void.

I know I didn't have what my siblings enjoyed,
Yet, I smiled in every family photo and "happy daughter"
Polaroid.

Now all pictures with her I have to avoid,
Because existing in her fantasy life and mock family has left
me perpetually annoyed.

She conned me into thinking that she could be that kind of
mother,
And I tricked her into thinking that I could be that type of
permissive daughter.

With my questions and issues she refused to bother,
But as I aged, living in her insanity only became harder and
harder.

As the emotional distance between us got farther and farther,
A good mother-daughter relationship I learned not to ponder.

Everyone is quick to blame my father,
But the real problem has always, always been my mother

She refused to be that kind of mother to me,
So that kind of daughter I vowed never again to be.

265

I want you to know that I love and appreciate you
I don't personally know you
But I love you
I know exactly what you have been through
And because of our shared mother-daughter pain
I have an undying connection with you
And I know how your own mother has manipulated and used
and mistreated you
She's the problem dear daughter
It happened to me too

Her misery and self-hatred for herself has nothing to do with you
It would have continued all my days until I boldly decided that I wouldn't allow it to
No contact was the only thing I had left to do
That and this book for you
There is nothing you have said and there isn't anything you could do
Life without her abuse and lies and drama has been beautiful
Her insanity and evil have absolutely nothing to do with you
She just doesn't really love or give a crap about you
And you and I have years and years of proof
Some mothers just can't be persuaded into caring about you
And evil and heartless mothers will never love and accept you
They are purposely mean and constantly say wicked and untrue things about you
Although none of it is true
But you still survived when she turned her back on you
We still pulled through
So let us help the other adult daughters too
Because in me, I want other struggling daughters to also see you
I'm proud of you for going no contact with that cruel woman and her band of crazy fools
I know how they tried to also manipulate and intimidate you
So as she goes down in flames in this book
They're going down too because they refused to allow us to unhook
Her enablers are totally responsible too
I'm taking down anyone who didn't make demands on your behalf and didn't defend you
Hey, an adult daughter has to do what a daughter has to do
It's too late to apologize once we come for you
"Family" shall go down too
Through our writings and our voices we are coming for you
Once this book is out there will be nothing you can do
And any person who has a problem with what I write or say or do
Let me be the first to say calmly, "Oh, fuck you!"

How we choose to deal with the evil mothers in our lives is about us
It ain't got shit to do with you
In this book we're taking down her Terracotta Warriors and her minions too
Because being on the wrong side of justice means that you have to held responsible too
And like a Saddam statue in Firdos Square eventually comes down too
Anyone who shielded her from her responsibilities to her daughter we're knocking down too
It's great being us right now
But it is about to really, really suck being you
Ha, new rules!

### 266

Who would want that kind of criticalness around?
Daughter, her negativity deliberately aims to intentionally bring you down,
And we cringe every time we hear she'll be visiting our town.

I think she secretly wants you to stumble and fail,
She calls herself your mother, but she makes it so very hard to tell.

For us, her Christian and holy-roller act is a tough sell,
Because we know the real her oh too well.

She treats you as if your decisions are always flawed and your wisdom is somehow frail,
And her evil behavior is excused by others when they say,
"Oh, you know she means well."

When a mother trades in her angel wings for horns,
When repercussions and consequences are immanent for her I'm never torn.

She fights you like she has the supremacy of Jason Bourne,

But YOU are the wrong one when she gets YOU boiling and
you pop like kernels of corn.

You have learned to never revere or drink from her toxic
maternal well,
And you now realize that her words aren't as coveted as the
Holy Grail.

You are the daughter of a synthetic mother and you have a
unique story to tell,
You should have sung with Bob Marley as much as you've
wail.

Your relationship with her has clearly grown nightmarish,
moldy, and irrefutably stale,
She gleefully attacks you as she does so well
But to others there is a totally different and dishonest story she
tells
She acts innocent when she actually provoked your Billy Idol-
like *Rebel Yell.*

She is entangled in the judging and the cruel critiquing that
she does so well,
Your mother constantly searches for every teeny-weeny
imperfection on your exterior shell.

Under her intimidation, do not let your voice or boldness quell,
The minute she starts faultfinding, you should be prepared to
bail.

And as the anger in you starts to swell,
Remember that you are not alone and me and other
daughters understand your situation very, very well.

Say it anyway.
Daughter, it's your truth to tell,
When will they stop saying that she means well?
When will her minions stop saying it is spinach when we know
it is kale?

When will her Terracotta Warriors stop saying that the dusky
is actually pale?
When will her enablers stop saying that the front is really the
tail?
When will they stop reciting lies that have gotten overused and
grown stale?
It took decades for me to realize that I would never make her
bail
I'd just have to break out of her abusive jail
When will her idiots stop saying that she means well?
I mean, really, what the hell?
They buy every lie that that mean-ass woman tells
Our faux-families come to her defense by repeating her same
ole' tall-lying-ass-tales
But when it comes to honesty and truth they never walk that
trail
She and her Terracotta Warriors are never morally obligated
or ethically compelled
And the same tired excuse they use for her antics, they can
use for me as well
Just say, "Oh, she meant well"
Since that is the lie everyone in my family likes to tell.


267


I was never born to be her daughter
I was conceived to be her devotee
Her enslaved twin
Her mirror
Her genetic idol worshipper.


Upon me she projected all of her sadistic inner
She loves inflicting the burns and then will ask me how I got
the blister
She is always the saint and I'm always the sinner
She's always the uninformed finalist and I'm always the
beginner
I'm always the defeated and she is always winner
I'm always starving while she just had dinner

And no matter how good I look she says I could always be
thinner
A bit prettier.

Whatever decision I make she says that her ideas are always
better
Support or encouragement from her?
Hell, never!
Whatever my opinion is she categorizes her own faulty
thinking as greater
I've designed the life I want to live perfectly but she declares
that her fake lifestyle is better tailored
I'm always biting my tongue as she serves as my unrelenting
criticizer
She'll let me drown even though she has declared herself a
pious nautical sailor
My pain she loves to taste and savior
She is the type of self-absorbed mother that never-ever
returns the favor
She is ungrateful and she feels like she is owed something at
her very core
Her dubious nature and her false obligation always beg for
more
She is always, always condemning me to hell because her
jealousy and control issues and dishonesty comprises her
very core
Quick to insult another person's lifestyle when I saw her with
that woman behind that door
It is amazing that I can recall it all and I was only four
I asked my father when I got older and confirmed what I saw
She's a hypocrite who watches that woman's ass secretly
from afar
What her watch her as she drives the car
Hypocrites are always casting to hell what they actually are
I can remember it all and I was barely four.

I denied it for decades upon decades, but now I can finally
admit it
My mother is a faux-Christian-evil-hypocritical-phony-ass-
witch

I don't trust that chick!
She's wicked
I used to be afraid to answer my phone when it would ring
Because I knew she only wanted something
She never gave but was always taking, taking, taking
Borrowing money that I'd never again see
Taking from me money I earned and was needing
I NEVER borrowed anything
But I was made to feel like my faux-family and mother were somehow MY responsibility
And over the years her narcissistic mindset just got more and more upsetting.

It is hard for those who haven't experienced it to understand it
We try to explain it
But they don't get it
We cry and breathlessly try to explain the circumstances and depict it
But no matter how much we explain they'll never get it
The cruelty mothers inflict upon their daughters is constantly interwoven within it
And I know that many adult daughters who have suffered at the hands of their mothers can relate to it
So for us I write it.

268

In Fleetwood Mac's, *Rhiannon*
They sing that, "Players only love you when they're playing"
Well, I also think that some mothers only love their daughters when the daughter is obeying
Or the want something
Likely money
You know exactly what I'm saying
The apology and acknowledgment you are owed she'll never be paying
And for the increased stumbling blocks on your path she's always praying
Constantly hating

But she's the first person to claim that she knows exactly what
Jesus and everything in the Bible is saying
But you never believe any of the made-up stories and phony
insights she's relaying
Because her own immoral and disturbing life it's far too telling.

They say we, "shouldn't let our mothers get to us that way"
That easy for them to say
No one understands that we can't stop that constant evil
cerebral replay
The things that mean mother would do
Remembering all the critical and demented things she'd often
say
When all the witnesses were away
Her words of ridicule have always managed to stay
No matter how far away
Against me I know she prays
Because to her I am nothing more than prey
Wishing we could leave all the negative flashbacks in hidden
and singular place
Oh, how we wish the very memory of her could all be erased
All the time we spent trying to fix her was a waste
We scowl when she see her demonic photo in her Terracotta
Warrior's frame
Remembering all of those horrid flashbacks from this day or
that day
The events that she claims never even took place
We remember vividly every day
We try to stop the constant rumination but it happens anyway
She lies, lies, and lies and says that it never happened that
way
Always gas lighting denying the truth we say
For us the truth is necessary
For her lying is no only preferred
It's more than okay.

269

It's not just a generational thing
She doesn't respect our very being

Our happiness and success she's loathing
When we escape the horrors she's re-chaining
Her true and corrupt intentions are always gaining
Others won't accept what we're clearly seeing
They excuse what we are wisely knowing
Her Terra-Cotta Warriors will make excuses for her compulsive lying
And with her words there is no relying
A bunch of bullshit she's constantly supplying
Every word is dressed in a lie and every sentence she's deceptively styling
But to the unsophisticated she is somewhat appealing
She pretends to know but she's so very unknowing
And we know she is just fooling
Beware of her narcissistic brand of make-shit-up-as-I-go type of schooling
Never trust her sadistic mothering
A storm of daughter inspired honesty is finally ensuing
Her day of reckoning is already looming
She's always talking about how the sins of others lead to their eventual undoing
Then she should expect our ruling
Her phony and brutal reign is finally ending
And once this poetic "single" is published there will be no reviving
Because I'm finally telling.


270


The adult daughters are MY people.
I have a series of perfectionism problems that I'm working through
That's why I leave all errors in my books…it's true
When you were raised to act perfect it's really, really hard to allow my errors and flaws to be seen by you
Instead of focusing on what I did right I tend to focus and obsess over the written errors that (I think) make me look like a fool
Even though I know it's not true
Just like my mother taught me to do.

This was back when I thought that oral sex meant standing up
and talking about it
I mean, that's how oral book reports worked when I was a
child
So I thought that's how you performed it.

This was back when I cried when on the news they started
talking about fossil fuel
Because I thought that it was so sad that people were burning
dinosaur fossils for fuel
Yeah, I know, I thought that too.

This is back when I thought that a self-cleaning oven cleaned
itself
I thought robot arms would come out and start scrubbing or
something
Yikes, my young mind was really something else.

I was a kid so I didn't know a lot of things
But if there was one thing I was NEVER misreading
It's that my mother emotionally and psychologically mistreated
me
She treated me differently.

And decades later people would affirm for me
That they saw it too but never said anything
Then over twenty years later I asked my father and he was
actually candid and honest with me
He said,
"You're right, your mother never *really* liked you but she knew
that you were necessary"
And then he said,
"She wrongly thought that you'd somehow force me"
"I tried to get away but across states she followed me."

I have memories from three
I remember vividly

When she cornered her sister in the hallway and slapped her
in front of me
I remember her acting violently
I still remember what she was yelling
And from that moment on I knew that she wasn't who she
pretended to be
She was mean and angry
Scary
And I knew in my little brain that she was someone I shouldn't
be trusting.

Then my father proceeded to give me concreate examples
since infancy
Detailing the odd ways in which she'd even look at me
Completely detached and ornery
Only reinforcing for me that I was birthed to hold on to a man
always determined to leave
And eventually
I'd be catering to her instead of her caring for me
Once the parentification began I knew it was my job to keep
that woman happy
And nothing made her happier than materialism and money
So I kept it flowing
And although she was ungrateful
I kept spending
Not knowing that I was paying for something that was already
free
She was just withholding.

272

She treats you differently
Regularly
Religiously
You provide examples of proof and they still aren't believing
They're still doubting
Terracotta Warriors can be even more disturbing.

273

Emotionally neglected
Never protected
When I say it
No one can ignore it
It'll be widely syndicated.

## 274

The *real* her you can clearly see
And the *real* her isn't who she pretends to be
She pretends to be so caring and even artificially loving
But it's phony
She is a bad actress in her own twisted life story trying to win
a Tony
Daughters see what the audience is ignoring
Her life is a stage and she's always performing
The same lines for decades she's still reciting
The same ole' lies she keeps repeating
Familiar untruths she keeps telling
Dishonesty she keeps spreading.

It is best to doubt what she is saying
That show has been dead for many years
But the tickets she keeps selling
We know how the sequel ends but the same tale she never
stops remaking
And her secret jealousy and envy of her own daughter is even
more compelling
No one believes us even when it is the truth that we keep
retelling.

Adult daughters know what others dismiss and refuse to
acknowledge and see
She's envious of the fact that her daughter's own life is the
opposite of her evil mother's well-planned catastrophe
Her daughter is independent, self-reliant and tremendously
happy
Something her effed'up and envious mother never really
wanted her to ever be.

If you have brothers they often won't get it,
They'll act like they don't see it
Even some sisters will refuse to admit it
You have justifiably identified the faux-mother culprit
But they dismissively fail to understand why you can't handle
it.

Their lack of understanding has proven to be both
unsympathetic and inconsiderate,
And trying to explain yourself constantly only makes you
indignant.

Just the mere thought of being around her makes you feel
judged and insignificant,
Yet, to them, she is camouflaged as religiously all-knowing
and magnificent
Because they've bought and are hungrily eating her bullshit
Yeah, I said it.

You explain constantly to them that you have the same
mother, but a totally different parent,
But they still refuse to get it
Her actions are foreign to them, but to you, her devious ways
and intentional mistreatment of you is apparent.

You're just tired of defending yourself all of the damn time,
It is exhausting being permanently stationed on her firing line.

Yet, she is always getting away with it!
And although her devilish wrongdoings are apparent
Her Terracotta Warriors are always excusing and endorsing it
Our kinds of mother-daughter relationship pain ain't scripted
We know because we live it
Daughter, know that you are not alone in it
Adult daughters like us know the pain from a toxic mother-
daughter relationship
We understand it
Know that my mother is also narcissistic

And the pain and betrayal you feel
A zillion times I too have felt it
I too am a strong woman often reduced to tears over it
But I will no longer hide it
And there isn't a damn thing that her minions and Terracotta
Warriors can do to stop it
I will talk about it
And on these pages I am disclosing it
And like the East Compton Clovers and the Toro's
Best believe, all the way on, I'm most certainly bringing it!

### 276

Alas, my finest moment
On these pages, I am forever burying it
The pain we know
Adult daughters, we must try to somewhat reverse it
And stop other daughters from ever knowing it
And we must fight to never-ever repeat it
And what she did to us we must never-ever do it
I say, "I don't have a mother," when strangers ask about it
Because she is not owed nor deserves my testament
Over my life, my mother has no ownership
And her assertions should be deemed fraudulent
I will no longer allow her to take credit
I will no longer allow her to upset me nor cause me to panic
Your mother expects accolades for the basic stuff she did
I mean, simple and basic mother shit!
She wants a cookie for doing what a mother should do for her
kids!
I refuse to allow her to claim MY hard earned
accomplishments
Because my mother was too self-absorbed to even offer to
help
So, no, she can't have it!
I'm the ONLY one who worked for it
And she had very, very, very little to do with any of it
But narcissistic mothers are always stealing unearned credit.

To secure and protect my happiness and peace,

All conversations and interactions with them I also had to cease.
Off of Terracotta Warriors
Narcissistic mothers will constantly feed
Their weakness and their lack of awareness is her favorite feast
Daughter, no one is going to protect you and your wellbeing,
You have to do your own soul policing.


## 277

It's not just a generational thing
She doesn't respect our very being
Our happiness and success she's loathing
Her true and corrupt intentions are always gaining
Others won't accept what we're clearly seeing
Her Terracotta Warriors will make excuses for her compulsive lying
And with her words there is no relying
A bunch of bullshit she's constantly supplying
Every word is dressed in a deception and every sentence structure she's styling
To cover the shame and insecurities she herself is hiding
So, on paper we are screaming...and even crying
Because we acknowledge and fully accept what she has spent well over sixty years denying
It is nearly impossible to stop a liar from lying
We're done trying.

## 278

I've talked till my face turned blue
That evil woman still doesn't have a clue
And one of her minions had the nerve to ask me to
See the crap that I go through?
Instead of leaving it alone
See what her Terracotta Warriors will do?
It ain't NEVER her

It's ALWAYS you.

## 280

Ha, on what planet are those losers living?
See why the only option left was leaving?
She carries that Bible around but I know she ain't reading
Because if she was
She'd stop being evil and mistreating
The lies about me that she was spreading had me hitting the ceiling
Her dishonesty has never been to my liking
And her cruelties and judgments only led to more fighting
The dogma and sabotaging
The chastising
So I'm writing.

## 281

Not all adult daughters can smile
For us, we've never had a mother who'd walk that mile
Our lives
Even as adults
Is built around the happiness of her
Life is never-ever about us
Because we don't matter to her.


She'll do for others what she won't do for you
She'll borrow money from random suckers and say it is for you
Like she did when I was away at school
And if you gave her money thinking it was for me
Then you got fooled
She. Played. You.
Uh, the shady crap evil mothers will do!
They will lie, lie, lie and the daughters hold the proof
And the sadistic nature of a horrible mother is easy to see through
It's funny how her disloyalty constantly bleeds through
As she inflicts her Narcissistic Personality Disorder on to you

Oh, let me tell you all about what a vile "mother" like mine will
do.
She'll sabotage, betray, and lie on you
That's what my own mama likes to do
I have the type of mother that will surely try to ruin you.

<u>282</u>

The foundation for you has been laid
Be not afraid
In front of you there is a glorious and distinguished parade
Of accomplished and heroic adult daughters creating life their
way
Emotionally, psychically, and psychologically abused
daughters have something to say
Just because she's your mother doesn't make it okay
They'll tell you to be afraid
Your siblings may even try to tell you that your true feelings
shouldn't be on display
But say it anyway
Because there is no other way
Who she is and what she did never goes away
Her behavior and her unkind words are not okay
Our truth we will declare and proudly say
We will squash anyone who disagrees or gets in our one-way
lane
We will confront every deception and evil deed she mislaid
We refuse to take our unspoken and hidden stories to the
grave
Now, we will have our say!
Today!
Adult daughters will no longer allow our toxic mother-daughter
relationships to be our source of shame
We will face everything she has done and we will give her
crimes and offenses names
For telling the truth we shalt not be blamed
We will address the montage of issues she forbade
Our lives we will reclaim!
Within this book our pièce de résistance is inlayed
The price has already been paid.

Thousands of times I've looked into your eyes
The pain I see is similar to mine
And every day you look into the mirror, I too say, "Hi"
I'm you and you are I
We are two different adult daughters, but we feel the same
way inside
I suffer with you each time you swallow your pride
I too make an appearance with you when we both really just
want to hide
I'm with you each time no one takes your side
And I'm there when you go it alone
Because being honest for many is a very, very dangerous ride
My eyes swell also when you cry
I understand your triggers inside
We both have indistinguishable mothers
So I know what it's like
I know how hard you've tried
I know she's constantly combating your will to survive
For us their poisonous webs have been customized
In our brains her meanness has been crystalized.

284

"Keeping up with the Joneses" was my life
My parents were living way, way outside their means but
acted like the phoniness was justified
My mother has always had to have the biggest prize
Nothing had to actually be right
It just had to look nice
Yeah, it looked glamorous from the outside
But behind that iron gate the utilities are all cut off inside
Fake rich is how she's always liked to ride
Just like everything else
It was all a lie.

285

They say they are kin to me,
But inside those walls, there is no real trust or family-like
security.

The home is filled with illusions of grandeur,
Where the obedient daughter is expected to ignore the
mother's cruel and repeated slander.

The daughter has a grin on her face, but honestly she couldn't
be any madder,
Over the years, their relationship had become sadder and
sadder.

She lives in an illusionary world where the truth is drowned out
by spurious laughter,
There are insincere smiles and charlatan laugher to hide the
truth the girl is after.

They are a family that never, ever discusses what really and
truly matters,
Yet, her mother's coconspirators can't seem to understand
why it all ended in tatters.

Her parents and faux-family have always been faker than the
Mad Hatter,
But their toxicity will not stop her from reaching every goal
they tried to shatter.

### 286

She is the antithesis,
Maybe even my arch nemesis.

If I'm optimistic and hopeful,
She introduces the negative and puts my positive outlook into
a chokehold.

If I'm happy,
She reminds me to be a pessimist.

If I'm proud of myself,
Her criticisms never fail to make an appearance.

She may have given birth to me,
But everything else is meaningless you see.

Her multiple violations against me have been egregious,
Calling her "my mother" just seems utterly ridiculous.

I know all about her jealous deeds reaching beyond the
scandalous,
I just told my husband that I don't want her to ever again
visiting us.

No one can enter into our home who I don't trust,
Especially those with lying lips that are impossible to hush.

### 287

Her mother should be arrested and tried for all of her
conspiracies
For all of her daughter's emotional and mental killings
She sold her up the river time and time again for her mother's
faux-image and a few shillings
Yet, her daughter had the ovaries to speak up for herself when
no one else was willing.

### 288

She never provided a safe place for me to fail or land
Anger and resentment was ever present even with a Bible in
her hand

Our mother-daughter relationship had me feeling like I was
sinking in quicksand
Until I learned to stop adhering to her demands

Only I was willing to courageously admit that the image she
paraded to the world was a complete and utter sham

So when I'd grieve or share my situation, no one believed me
or really didn't gave a damn

To uphold her pious act, my lips remained closed and tighter
than a clam
Always relishing in the fact that she never supported me or
who I am

Unless she could take credit for it
Then she'd make my accomplishments a part of her sinister
plan
So as an adult, I found creative ways to distance myself and
live my life on the lamb

She stayed married to that pedophile and abuser and she
never-ever ran
She let him off the hook, yet I'd receive all of her irrational
theology rebukes and reprimands

I've officially done all I can
She will never, ever support or defend me over any man

She even tries explaining to me that my happiness in life isn't
actually part of God's plan
She thinks that my suffering somehow fulfills some sick goal of
hers and validates God's demands

So I've issued her a gold platted lifetime ban!
That's right.
Of her faux-religious psychosis, I am officially not a fan!

So, I've kicked her out of my group and I've started a new
band!
I was exhausted from making our dishonest and corrupt family
appear holy and glam
Especially after witnessing way too many of my parent's moral
scams.

## 289

It's funny how they don't believe you
Or they think that you exaggerate what you've been through
But I didn't have to be in there to believe you
Crimes like that are never committed in front of people
So when that indolent alibi is stated, I have a real issue

Especially since you, not them, was the one crying into the
tissue
We stand with you as they try to discredit your story too
Don't let the nonbelievers and your haters dictate what you will
or won't do
It's funny how contagious amnesia is and how people deny
the facts in favor of not having a clue

But don't let their repudiation or cruelty affect you
They may never understand that your honesty is the only
morally required proof
So I want you to know that we stand with you
And when your scars are internal, how do you submit proof?

They will likely act aloof,
But know that we got you!
When you've truthfully said and done all you can do,
Just send your truth deniers a heartfelt and sincere, "fuck
you!"
That's what I do.

## 290

They often treat the sons different from the daughters.
They love the boys,
But often lead the girls to the slaughter.

Your mother tried to stop everything that could make your life
better,
When your days got cold, that witch took your only sweater!

She even tried to disrupt your loving home and happy relationship,
But you were smart enough not to allow her to meddle in it.

I'm proud of you for not making that evil woman a factor,
And for your every wrong decision she was either the executer or the benefactor.

You once trusted her, but now you know better,
I can relate to you to the letter.

Now you can't even hear her complaining and negativity over your happiness and laughter,
We've finished the book on blissfulness and acceptance and she's never even read a single chapter.

### 291

As long as you know your purpose,
Stop trying to convince her that you are worth it.

You have already defeated your toxic family curses,
And you fought back when she and your siblings tried to make you feel worthless.

I am 100% behind you and we stand by your side,
It is okay to speak the truth they'd prefer that you not discuss in an effort to hide.

Don't you just hate that fake-ass family pride?
Rationalizing protecting them at your emotional expense is impossible to coincide.

I too am tired of being critiqued, misunderstood and mistreated,
Feeling forced to protect a dogmatic and faux-churchy family that only mirrors the wicked.

I have washed my hands of those idiotic fanatics,

Pretending to be decent people, when they are actually
hypocritical, unsupportive, sexist and erratic.

You have the right to excommunicate your relatives if you
need to,
They don't have the right to determine what is necessary for
you.

You alone must determine what you will do,
None of them have the right to make any decisions for you.

292

Your mother is an emotional recidivist
A psychological terrorist
But we survived
I'm proud of us.

293

She's self-centered and is always "me, me, me"
It ain't never about how you feel about anything
A mother who doesn't really care is never even asking
They're never loving
They're never understanding
They're never helping
Never listening
Never empathizing
But is always prepared to through insults and begin criticizing.

294

Girl, you're as adorable as the Puppy Bowl
Cuter than the halftime kitten show
And I'd miss you if you didn't go

Your mother rather insult you and offer backhanded
compliments than to tell you so
But you are a truly beautiful and kind soul
Inside and out I want you to know
Read this reminder when your mean and jealous mother tries
to make you feel low
Don't you dare internalized her low blows
And just because your evil-ass mother said it
Doesn't make it so.

### 295

The song *Mother Knows Best* from the movie *Tangled*
She'll point out all the demons when you're searching for
angels.

She'll try to eat your soul like the Other Mother did *Coraline*
While trying to trap you and attempting to coerce you into
putting buttons over your eyes.

Like the mother in Ingmar Bergman's "Autumn Sonata" sadly
You share your tragedies and she'll make it all about me, me,
me.

### 296

We have living mothers with dead hearts
She's a car with no engine so for you it'll never start
Although she throws out insults  à la carte
I could never tear you apart
And realizing that our mothers will never change is the hardest
part

Being her daughter is like trying to win a prize every day at the hardest and most impossible game in the entire amusement park.

<u>297</u>

She's like the grandmother in the short horror film *SLUT*
Your feelings, your challenges, and your day doesn't really interest her much
I'd walk in with my back erect and head up
But after an hour with her at lunch
I'd end up walking out feeling defeated through those doors with my posture hunched.

<u>298</u>

I could always depend on my mother to make a bad situation worse for me
She NEVER had any sympathy, empathy - - nothing
And she did this consistently
She's late for everything
But she arrives bright and early when it comes to attacking me
She'd always play the victim but I was the one crying
I was the one lied on but guess who her Terracotta Warriors were always consoling
"Well, you know how she is" or "she doesn't mean any harm" they were always saying
Her calculated cruelties they were always excusing
And once I started standing up for myself she made me the scapegoat for everything
The lies she's spread about me are truly horrifying
Always out to make me look like I'm completely crazy
Then turn right around and ask me for some money

And I use to give it to her
Like a dummy.

## 299

I was a teenager back then
In a dressing room right next to them
So it was easy to hear them
And I heard this girl's mother criticizing her loudly for not being
thin
The Contempo sales girl kept bringing outfits again and again
And I'd heard the daughter compliment herself and in her
voice I could hear her grin
And I heard her mother say, "those were cute until you got in"
"Gross, you look like I could pop your stomach with a pin"
And when I heard her mother stepped out
I quickly went next door and knocked and whispered and the
daughter let me in
And when I came in she was in tears
And I hugged her and I told her that I understood the
emotional hell she was living in
We had two totally different colors in our skin
But the EXACT same boat of mother-induced-misery we were
both in
I told her that just because her mother walks around with that
crucifix on don't make her no Christian
And I told her that one day I'll write my book and what
happened to her I'll mention
And other daughters like us will understand and the world will
listen
Her mother said she'd be back in five minutes so I didn't even
get her name
But I hope she's readin'.

Edgar Allan Poe and Janet Jackson both had a *Black Cat*
And I have one right now in my lap
People learn the hard way that it's best for me to purr and not
scratch
Because I'll draw blood if I have to fight back
And when it comes to my husband, Jeff Bezos/Amazon,
Stephen King, and The Black Cat Daughters
Talk negatively about any of them and my claws become
impossible to retract
And I go on the attack!
But before I pounce
I'd strongly suggest that whoever said it had better take it back
Because when I get angry no fragile ego is left intact
And when it comes to those who've instrumentally helped me
It's impossible for me to ever overreact
And yeah, it's really like that
The world ain't seen nothing yet.


# BLACK CAT

Made in the USA
San Bernardino, CA
10 June 2018